An Introduction to
Early English Law

Bill Griffiths

Anglo-Saxon Books

Published by
Anglo-Saxon Books
Frithgarth
Hockwold-cum-Wilton
Norfolk, England

First Published 1995
Reprinted 1998 - 2000 - 2003

British Library Cataloguing-in-Publication Data. A catalogue
record for this book is available from the British Library.

ISBN 1–898281–14–9

FOREWORD

There is no full picture of the practical working of Old English Law. Much of Anglo-Saxon life must have followed a traditional pattern, of custom, and of dependence on kin-groups for land, support and security. The Viking incursions of the ninth century and the reconquest of the north that followed both disturbed this pattern and led to a new emphasis on centralised power and law, with royal and ecclesiastical officials prominent as arbitrators and settlers of disputes. The merits of a case could be discussed at the shire court, or established by oath, or assessed by the degree of financial surety offered in support, or by the backing of prominent patrons; in other cases, a ritual ordeal would be used to establish guilt or innocence; in yet bitterer disputes, direct vengeance (the blood feud) remained likely, though legislation provided for a 'cooling-off' period, and almost any offence could be settled by paying compensation – but this in turn could well involve slavery for the poorer man called to account.

This diversity and development is sampled here by selecting several law-codes to be read in translation – that of Ethelbert of Kent, being the first to be issued in England, Alfred the Great's, the most clearly thought-out of all, and short codes from the reigns of Edmund and Ethelred the Unready.

CONTENTS

INTRODUCTION

Although written Law is now a universal element in complex societies, a definition of what it is not easy to supply. W. H. Auden's "Law is only crimes / punished by places and by times"[1] is a fair warning against accepting too readily abstractions centring on Justice and Natural Morality[2] – for that attempts to give positive meaning to a process that is essentially negative. Rather, a law-code might be defined as a set of negative precepts, enforceable in retrospect by penalties supervised by a central authority[3]. Like many aspects of Western life we take for granted, a closer analysis shows a complex historical development rather than a 'steady state'; and though modern British Law somewhat

---

[1] From his poem 'Law Like Love' (1939).

[2] Thus in the Breviary of Alaric: 'Quid sit lex: Lex est emula divinitatis, antestis religionis, fons disciplinarum, artifex iuris, boni mores inveniens adque componens, gubernaculum civitatis, iustitie nuntia, magistra vite, anima totius corporis popularis. Quare fit lex: Fieri autem leges hec ratio cogit, ut earum metu humana coerceatur inprobitas, sitque tuta inter noxios innocentium vita, atque in ipsis inprobis formidato supplicio frenetur nocendi presumptio' (1,2) – which may be loosely translated: "What should Law be? Law is the image of the godhead, the demonstration of religion, the source of correct behaviour, the author of propriety, revealing and confirming good behaviour, the rudder of the state, the herald of justice, the mistress of life, the soul of the whole civic body. Why is Law necessary? These arguments support the forming of laws: that evil-doing be restrained by human fear of their operation, and that the life of innocent people be made safe among many dangers, and that the intention to harm is curbed in any evil-doer by the likelihood of fearful retribution."

[3] Wormald, 1977, p.107, more exactly defines Anglo-Saxon legislation as "written decrees by secular authority with ostensible general application" – to distinguish (secular) law from private charter and ecclesiastical legislation ('canons').

denies its Anglo-Saxon sources,[4] yet the sort of law-codes presented in this study are undoubtedly the original source of Law in this country,[5] and in turn reflect late- and post-Roman practices in Europe.

The elements contributing to Anglo-Saxon Law may be analysed as follows:

(a)   tribal or popular custom;

(b)   the Romano-Christian tradition of writing out and codifying information;

(c)   the growth of central authority – 'kingship';

(d)   abstract or moral ideals.

To give more detail, German scholars of the 19th century were inclined to stress the early 'barbarian' laws as a product of national will and popular sentiment, making of it a prototype for democratic developments in their own period.[6] The view of Anglo-Saxon society as a band of equal freeman is attractive,[7] but may conveniently be relegated to the mists of an epic past, for the purposes of this introduction. For the period of recorded history, an Anglo-Saxon king

---

[4]   Legal memory in this country extends no further back than the coronation of Richard I in 1189; Maitland (1957, p.98) regarding law, notes "a singular continuity from Alfred's day to our own".

[5]   It has to be admitted, though the importance of law texts in the Anglo-Saxon period is self-evident, and should form the basis not only of any study of the history of law, but also of the history of government, they are now amongst the least popular of texts in Old English. They seldom have any pretension to literary style; but though their language is relatively simple, the condensed style and presence of many technical terms do not recommend the texts to beginners. The overt cruelty of some of the provisions, and their sometimes seeming absurdity (to modern ears) may incline us to doubt the practical role of such laws – but the adjustment needs to be made in our understanding of the context, not in the texts themselves. Perhaps we are made uneasy by the possibility that modern Law has not sufficiently left behind these very characteristics.

[6]   See Wormald, 1977, pp.109–11.

[7]   Is it this that supplies some of the appeal of the poem *The Battle of Maldon*, and imbues with a special quality of adventure the early exploits of Beowulf?

was chosen out of a small group of eligible contenders by election,[8] involving the more privileged members of the community, and then imbued with the abstraction of power by some mark of Church approval – a ritual anointing, by the time of Edgar (973), implying a quasi-priestly role.[9] As there was some element of acclamation or general consent in the appointment of a king, so too some element of consent was sensible in a law-code, and it seems to have been usual for approval of law-codes to be sought at a Witan[10] – perhaps also some expression of opinion was permitted.

---

[8] Usually from the established family – 'cyning' as arising from 'kin' – all members of that family possessing in theory 'throne-worthiness' (Kern 1939 p.12), an 'inheritance-identity' reinforced by genealogies, going back to major ancestors like Woden, perhaps implying ancestor-worship. But what exactly family descent implied is not clear – some sort of intangible 'mana' or passing on of status or personality may be indicated by the alliterative chaining of names in a genealogy (and see fn.16, below). Primogeniture – descent as of right to the eldest son – only became a firm concept in England after the Norman Conquest, where it helped keep large feudal estates intact. In Germanic society (as in Roman Law) division of property amongst the heirs was the norm – see Whitelock, 1952, p.153 – which reinforced the kin system, since relatives had to co-operate in managing the common property. But the claim of the eldest son, followed by the next eldest and so on is implicit in Alfred's eventual attainment of the crown, suggesting that the advantages of an ordered succession were appreciated quite early. Yet changes of dynasty did occur, and cases of deposition – thus Alcred of Northumbria was deposed by "counsel and consent of all his people" (Loyn, 1960, p.51), and conversely, in 759 a non-royal contender claimed the throne "a sua plebe electus" (*Continuatio Bedae*).

[9] Anointing or unction in the West may go back to the 6th century (Kern, 1939 p.34); it was accepted twice by Pippin (751, 754) who needed reinforcement of his (usurped) royal position; in England perhaps Offa of Mercia's designation of his son Ecgferth as successor, by a ritual of anointing, is the first example. Anointing is based on the precedent of Saul and David in the Old Testament, and in Anglo-Saxon times was considered to confer the "sevenfold gifts of the Holy Spirit" (Kern, 1939 p.37), so that the recipient became transformed, rather as did a priest, into "an adoptive son of God" (Kern 1939, p.37).

[10] "A purely aristocratic gathering" as Davis, 1913, p.429, notes; from Ine's time an "aristocratic *élite* created by the monarchy" (F. Liebermann *The*

Again, there is an undoubted percentage of customary or traditional material in Anglo-Saxon law-codes[11] looking back to the sort of (?self-) regulation any tribe or consciously defined group might need to function;[12] and that not always the simplest provision. Thus, the detailed scales for settlement of injury by payment may not be a Christian intervention to moderate the action of the feud, for "the principle of compensation is an inherent part of any feuding system",[13] and is already remarked on by Tacitus.[14] On such tariffs of injury, Witney remarks:[15] "If much of this now seems rather ludicrous, it illustrates how sensitive this society was to considerations of mere dignity, and how easily a trivial brawl could flare up into a feud unless damped down at once by some satisfaction…"

National Assembly in the Anglo-Saxon Period (New York, 1913, p.20), though an 'aristocracy' by birth (i.e. not by royal appointment) may be implied in Hlothhere and Eadric's Laws. Wulfstan's *Institutes of Polity* define such a Council as "cyning and bisceopan, earlan and heretogan, gerefan and deman, lar-writan and lah-witan"; but a Kentish letter in Athelstan's time (Liebermann 1,170) claims to involve bishops, thegns, eorls *and* ceorls; and London ordinances (VI Athelstan, Prologue and §§3, 7, 8) give the common people a role of assent, almost "as though they were *de jure* the source of law." (Davis, 1913, p.429). Richards 1989 p.11 notes that OE 'we' is used in the Laws, perhaps to imply the "collected wisdom of the king and his councillors."

[11] There would be an advantage in basing a law-code on traditional material, for as Drew (1972, p.3) notes: "[*mos*, customary law] has a moral force enhanced by social acceptance and as such cannot conscientiously be ignored as is often the case with regard to man-made law, which requires an agent of enforcement." Hanging, while rarely mentioned in the law-codes, was one aspect of traditional punishment that continued in use, with clearly a ritual if not a sacrificial significance (cf. early Roman penalties).

[12] Necessary indeed if we take too literally Loyn's (1960, p.92) "impression that the Anglo-Saxons devoted much of their time to inflicting injuries upon each other."

[13] Wormald, 1977, p.111. In a sense, OE laws reduce every offence to 'theft', for which a monetary equivalent can be found.

[14] *Germania* c.12.

[15] 1982, p.96.

While Wormald[16] makes a plea for the enduringly oral nature of Anglo-Saxon Law, with texts of codes "something in the nature of minutes of what was orally decreed, rather than statute law in their own right," it has to be affirmed that such law-codes depend necessarily on the affinity for writing and codifying typical of the Romano-Christian tradition.[17] Without written form, there is not Law but custom, taboo, etc.[18] It is a matter of status also: "The provision of a written law-code was a sign, like the adoption of Christianity, that Kent had joined the more advanced Germanic kingdoms of Europe."[19] And of course text has its mystical aspects – of exact, repeated, powerful words, of fixity and authority, as though some universal design lies behind mere created pattern. But it is a practical matter also: the advantages in putting texts into (relatively) fixed form and analysing, organising and developing them must have been as attractive to the Anglo-Saxons as the computer is to any modern researcher or administrator.

Without any known class of society dedicated to formulating or reciting Law[20], the scribe or ecclesiastical adviser may have played a more important part in the construction of Law at this time than is obvious from the law-codes themselves.[21] The King is the nominal producer of the Law, but in, for example, Alfred's Preface, clearly

---

[16] 1978, p.48.

[17] Runes, designed for carving, do not seem to have been considered suitable for extended texts, so Anglo-Saxon pre-Christian tradition remained an oral matter. (An exception is the Norse 'Laws of Skåne' in the Danish Codex Runicus AM 28, written down in runes, perhaps as a sort of historical affectation.) Generally, parchment, pen and Roman alphabet were adopted together as one system; and with it came an established tradition concerning the lay-out and content of laws.

[18] Thus Germanic Law "was essentially customary law – the traditions or customs handed down by word of mouth for untold generations in the past." Drew 1988.

[19] Yorke, 1990, p.41.

[20] Though note brief poetic references on this assembled by Whitelock, 1952, at p.135. A law-speaker is noted in later Norse sagas, while a literary class preserving oral literature and laws is assumed for Ireland – see Myles Dillon and Nora Chadwick *The Celtic Realms* (London, 1973) pp.259–60.

[21] Thus, the Church is assessed to have had a "powerful" influence "on the language, structure, and style of the legal codes." (Richards, 1989, p.5).

ecclesiastical theory plays a major role in the text, and Archbishop Wulfstan himself drafted some of the laws of Ethelred and Cnut.[22] The texts of laws, similarly, would be copied in monastic scriptoria,[23] so that the Church provided not only the concept and some contribution, no doubt, to the content, but the means of preservation, multiplication and distribution.

The third element, kingship, is a regularisation of traditional tribal leadership, by introducing concepts of legitimacy,[24] special authority, scope of power, purpose etc., that establish the king in a unique and advantageous position, in turn encouraging further centralisation and larger administrative areas, bringing more people into the process of government as deputies, and so inducing more stability.[25] Customary law thus becomes transformed into 'active' law i.e. new custom or precedent for the future.[26] It is from the king that all known Anglo-Saxon law-codes emanate, and as the size of such kingdoms increase, so the law-codes become more ambitious in their scope, as though (practical considerations apart) they are a necessary annexe of growing royal status.[27]

An added impetus, it needs to be remembered, is that in taking on the central regulation of justice, the King was able to levy fines[28] in

---

[22] Similarly, Dunstan is thought to have drafted 4 Edgar, for example, and Archbishop Berhtwald to have assisted Wihtred of Kent.

[23] For example for distribution to eorls, reeves, etc. – see Whitelock, 1952, p.137. This process of distribution is specifically mentioned at the end of 4 Edgar.

[24] See footnote 8, above.

[25] For details of the process of "state formation", see *The Origins of Anglo-Saxon Kingdoms* ed. Steven Bassett, Leicester 1989.

[26] As Drew (1988) notes re the Lex Burgundionum. I develop this aspect further, below.

[27] Arguably, in the reigns of Edward and Athelstan the increased royal power, by conquest in effect, was reflected in a lower status for all freemen, who become subject to testing by ordeal, an apparent contradiction of the principle that physical injury is the treatment accorded a slave but freemen would be exempt from such (see Alfred, Laws, ch.35).

[28] This was not an Anglo-Saxon invention. The Lex Burgundionum included both compensation to be paid to the victim and a fine to the king's treasury. In practice perhaps a percentage of such a fine would be paid to informers,

addition to any compensation paid to the victim, and this enabled Law to be used as a source of government income.[29] But he could not be expected to administer the Law personally, except perhaps for appeals, special cases or those occurring within his immediate notice.[30] A law-code thus implies a system of Courts, however simple, and some sort of shire administration[31] becomes a necessary adjunct of Law, and is deemed to have been in place by Athelstan's reign. Local hundred Courts also came into use[32] and some provision of safe custody.[33] However, with no central 'prosecution' service and no juries,[34] the

---

though this is only specifically stated in Ine's Laws ch.17 ('meld-feoh'). By contrast, a fine is only mentioned twice in the earlier laws of Ethelbert, nor are 'reeves' (King's officers) mentioned in that early code.

[29] Loyn, 1960, p.81, summarises as follows: "The kings were not motivated by an innate sense of justice and desire for orderly government; they were primarily interested in a strong law and order because it brought peace and unity to their realm, gave them military strength, and produced a steady flow of income into the royal chamber."

[30] One petitioner recalls catching Alfred as he was washing his hands (The Fonthill Letter, *English Historical Documents* no.102). This sort of informality is specifically excluded in 2 Edmund and 3 Edgar, where appeals to the king are only permitted when local procedures have been exhausted.

[31] "A set of statutes is valueless until it has authority behind it," as Whitelock sensibly notes (1955, p.77). Shires were apparently in place in Wessex by about 800; the shire court would be superintended by an ealdorman and a bishop – see Richards, 1989 p.4.

[32] By the mid 10th century – see discussion in *English Historical Documents* re item 39. Loyn (1992, pp.112–4) notes the possible origin of the Hundred as a Carolingian administrative unit; the Hundred Court, presided over by someone who could well be a king's reeve, may have owed its origin to some sort of popular local assembly.

[33] Corresponding to the modern concept of remand in custody? There does not seem to be any attempt to use prison or detention as a standard punishment, for of course the gaoler is likely to end up paying for board and lodging, a possibility guarded against in for example Alfred's Laws 1, 5.

[34] The possible use of the king's reeve as investigator and executioner, even, occurs only so late as 1 Ethelred. Juries are first mentioned in Ethelred's Wantage code as appropriate to the Danelaw. These were juries of 'presentment', i.e. in the role of witnesses rather than arbitrators. Wormald, 1978, pp.66–8, argues that the jury might derive as much from Carolingian

functioning of law depended on the initiative of individuals (rather as Civil Law does today), while guilt and innocence were attested by the sort of backing in terms of financial guarantees a person could assemble, by the provision of supporting oaths[35] or simply judgement by ordeal.[36] None of these is absolutely capable of providing proof, and while many aspects of Anglo-Saxon Law did develop tremendously, they never seem to have moved far away from the small-society concept that the doer of a deed must be obvious to all, and that local suspicion is tantamount to proof.

That might be an adequate basis for justice in a close-knit community, where everyone knew the whereabouts and actions of others, and most disputes could be settled openly between equals by precedent or arbitration (with a few serious, thus especially 'secret', crimes being exempted from settlement and meriting direct retaliation or outlawry). But in the more complex, extended, less settled and more

---

'Inquisitio' procedure as from Viking custom. The modern concept of jury as random opinion may owe something to 19th century regard for Greek use of chance appointments as an element of democracy.

[35] "In Anglo-Saxon courts there was no assessment of evidence but rather an assessment of oaths. A man swore that a charge was true or false and if necessary produced a number of his kinsmen or fellows to support his oath as compurgators or oath-helpers." (Kirby, 1967, p.144). In short, evidence as to the character (and in some measure status) prevails.

[36] There is an early, but unclear, reference to ordeals in Ine ch.37, 62, on which see Attenborough pp.187–9, where there are extensive notes on the practice in general. Ordeals are first emphasised in Edward's reign, seemingly as a sort of rough justice for those who could not manage otherwise to assert their innocent status; to some extent they may have been used to circumvent the understanding (e.g. in Alfred Laws ch.35) that a freeman would not be subject to corporal punishment. They come into prominence in Athelstan's reign and by 1 Ethelred are applicable to freeman and slave alike. Ordeals were administered by the Church, and intended to reveal the judgement of God, but in practice they were a test of endurance – an element not lacking in the modern trial process?

An even simpler method was available in Frisia: a set of lots would be kept in a reliquary or an altar, and the accused would select either a blank lot or one marked with a cross, revealing his guilt or innocence. See Albin Saupe *Der Indiculus Superstitionum* (Leipzig)

centralised society emerging after Alfred's death, this ethic no longer applies, except as a fictional ideal. It was not so much the local community as the royal officer who needed to be satisfied, and to this end a demonstration of guilt was necessary. That the means of achieving this seem to us unsatisfactory reflects our belief that we can now *prove* rather than simply *demonstrate* guilt.

It also implies an emerging concept of personal responsibility, that needs some further explanation. The idea of guilt, with each human possessing a soul and thus in control of his or her actions, is arguably an ecclesiastical rather than a legal concept by origin. The modern grading of intent, contributory negligence and non-responsibility were only shadowy concepts at the start of our period.[37] Compensation itself would be collectable from and payable to a kin-group rather than an individual, suggesting communal responsibility. For whatever reason, this seems less workable or less acceptable in the tenth century, and increasing dependence is placed on the ordeal and individual penalties.

But for how long and how widely did royal justice apply? – for the association of a king with a law-code raises the question of how valid such a code would have been after the king's life-time. This seems to be the point raised in the Fonthill Letter, where a judgement of Alfred is being disputed after his death. Yet the Laws of Edward seem to be supplementary to Alfred's, which remains the "dom-boc" still in force. Did Alfred intend Ine's Laws to be published with his and to supplement his own? Conversely, would large-scale changes in Law indicate a breach of continuity, for whatever purpose? In general, it seems most recent law took precedence, but previous law might also be valid where it amplified doubtful points or filled gaps.[38] As to how widely a law-code applied, there was clearly some intention (e.g. Edward and Guthrum) to apply West Saxon standards to the Danelaw, but this can only have had a chance while Wessex controlled the north – something it did not do consistently in the tenth century. Curiously, the

---

[37] "Ancient criminal law knew only the concept of harm. Crime and guilt, occupying such an eminent place in modern criminal law, were absent at this stage of development. Conscious, careless and accidental actions were evaluated exclusively by their consequences." *Pashukanis: Selected Writing on Marxism and Law* ed. P. Beirne and R. Sharlet (London, 1980) p.118.

[38] This is discussed in Richards, 1986.

Viking word 'lagu' for law seems eventually to have prevailed over Old English alternatives.

The fourth and final element I propose is the least tangible: a moral or ethical direction i.e. that Law is not only the preservation of peace and order (at a practical level via a central authority) but the embodiment of important assumptions concerning right and wrong (as commonly conceived or taught at any time) and so, by extension, has an improving or reforming purpose as well, moving society closer to a (Christian) ideal. "The *Leitmotif* of all ecclesiastical political theory is the dictum: What is right, ought to be law. The state, in this view, exists for the purpose of transforming ethical rightness into binding positive law."[39] In this sense, Law is 'pivotal' – for it is at that delicate balanced central point where the ideal, as it were, is made textual and actual, with the potential of influencing and shaping events as well as remedying the past. This is more apparent in law-codes from Edgar's reign onwards: King and Church are no longer merely practical administrators but aware of their potential in shaping the future too.[40]

In this sense the Laws are in part abstract collections, with the dual function of display and use, indicating a king's intention to uphold justice and order, giving detail, and uniting the process by the ideal of improvement. But it may then seem that content is irrelevant, if laws act at levels other than the purely practical.[41] Certainly, the Old English

---

[39] Kern, 1939, p.28. Richards (1989, p.7) notes that the Prefaces of II Edmund and X Ethelred specifically aim to promote Christian values.

[40] Perhaps Law operates also at a level of concept of what reality (from the root 'royal') should be as well as at a practical level, and by setting out what is unacceptable, give us an inverse definition of the values subtending reality. From this a sense may arise that what is prohibited by law must be occurring, as in 17th century witchcraft trials. Taken to its extreme, there seems also a sense in which laws not only define, but publicise, almost stimulate (dare I say?) the behaviour they are intended to discourage – a criticism made, for example, of current Crimewatch-type programmes on TV.

[41] Thus Wormald (1977, p.122) having examined charters that mention legal proceedings finds not one direct reference to the provision of any law-code (cf. Wormald 1978, p.48). He concludes (1977, p.135) that 'lex scripta' is "not so much practical as ideological," and more emphatically (1978, p.49) that "early medieval legal texts are mere clerical fantasies, without relevance

Laws do not permit us, strictly, to re-create a picture of contemporary life from its content, but this would be so with most sets of statutes. In fact, most Old English law-codes begin by stressing the special status of King and Church, that is indicating the origin of hierarchy. Beyond that the minimisation or control of violence is a central concern, perhaps to bring about a more peaceful orderly society, or to channel the potentially excessive or emotive operation of kin-backed feuds,[42] or perhaps just to encourage the centralisation of the right to action. Next, property figures prominently in the laws; not so much the control of land, which could be communal rather than private, except for bookland owners and for tenants (both these figure in charters), but more often in terms of 'mobile' items such as cattle, and personal items such as artefacts and slaves. In this way the laws reflect approval of the accumulation of wealth, and by reinforcing a settled long-term concept of status, act to satisfy all levels of free society where custom had not provided adequate guidance, but with only limited safeguards in place for the less advantaged.

For in practice, justice must have depended very much on status. The slave is sometimes mentioned in the laws[43] but was generally liable to

---

to the law as it was issued and enforced in Anglo-Saxon England." "Their existence as books was what mattered most," Wallace-Hadrill comments (1971, p.37).

[42] A prominent theme in the later Icelandic Saga of Burnt Njal, where feud of itself is shown to grow and grow, without any moderating influence. "An insult, although committed in retribution, itself becomes the basis for a new feud," *Pashukanis: Selected Writings* ed. P. Beirne and R. Sharlet (1980) p.111. Originally, the intention was that the threat of retaliation would act as a restraining influence, thus "the kindred itself was a law-enforcing institution" (Kirby, 1967, p.141) and OE *sibb* means both 'kinship' and 'peace'. However, the idea of hot-blooded revenge without a rational element cannot have appealed to Christian rulers – thus the analysis in Alfred ch.42.

[43] Not always as a measure of protection; a Latin code (4 Athelstan) prescribes stoning to death as the punishment for a male slave for theft, burning to death for a female slave; while 3 Edmund c.4 requires a thieving slave to be scalped ('extoppentur' in the Latin); such rigour may have inspired Ælfric to warn against taking Old Testament concepts too literally, in the Preface to his translation of Genesis. For a more optimistic survey of slavery in this

17

whatever penalty his or her master cared to apply, on top of the already existing duty of labour.[44] Consequently the loss of free status was the greatest sanction that could be used to moderate behaviour, for it not only removed a person from direct access to the Law, but took away the rewards of personal labour. A freeman could in theory atone for any crime by paying compensation, but in practice he must often have been unable to raise the fine and so lost his freedom.[45] In theory a full member of society, it is likely, especially later in the period, that he may have been more in the role of a client to a local notable[46] than absolutely independent, and so accountable through as well as supported by such a liege lord when it came to a dispute in law. A dispute with a powerful magnate could lead to ruthless retribution, as in the case of the sack of Dover, reported in the *Chronicle* for 1051.

Yet the Old English Laws are more, too, than a display or a commentary on existing custom. For if individual articles are

---

period see Loyn 1992, ch.14; slavery as a status had fallen into virtual disuse by the later 12th century.

[44] And, apparently, of procreation. Thus the discussion in Alfred's Pref. ch.11.

[45] The practice of penal slavery ('witeðeow') is mentioned as early as Ine ch.24; this could imply not only forced labour in one's own country but selling abroad for profit (as in Wihtred's code, see Witney 1982, p.166) – something forbidden in Ine ch.11. Servitude as a punishment when the cost of settlement cannot be raised is further confirmed in 2 Edward. In general the laws seem to evidence a decline in the meaningfulness of free status from the early 10th century onwards, paralleling the rise of centralised power.

[46] "Law dealt more readily with lords than with kindreds," Loyn (1992, p.59) notes. Hence the tendency to accentuate membership of a guild or tithing (6 Athelstan) as a substitute for kin (perhaps envisaged as early as Ine's Laws, see Kirby, 1967, p.143), and the frequent insistence in 10th century laws that the lord be accountable for the actions of his men, and choose them carefully. Loyn (ibid., pp.62–3) notes that kin institutions developed more fully in the weakly-centralised Celtic and Scandinavian lands than in England, where the monarchy always acted as a counter-force. On the question of later influence from lay magnates, Wormald (1978, p.69) doubts if there was any substantial privatisation of justice in the tenth or eleventh centuries i.e. with fines going to the owner of a court rather than the king; but see also Loyn, 1992 p.133 and Goebel, 1973 ch.6.

considered, it must often appear that within an apparently detailed provision with little general interest or use, ideas of responsibility are implied that have a much wider relevance. Thus when Alfred (Intro. ch.21) quotes Exodus on the risks of being gored by an ox, a concept of responsibility on the owner's side is being laid down, which is then applied in his Laws proper (ch. 23) in the case of a dangerous dog, and might thence be quoted, presumably, in any case that involved attack by a kept animal[47] – the test points being whether the owner knew it to be dangerous and whether he took any steps to restrain it. Ine (ch.43) holds the lighter of a fire responsible for consequent damage "for fire is a thief", that is a destroyer or remover of property, an equation affirmed in Alfred ch.12; but an accidental death during tree-felling (Alfred ch.13) is not considered to involve that level of responsibility. In the case of the angle at which a spear is to be carried (Alfred ch. 36), it is being asserted that some concept of risk applies, and that if someone acts in such a way as to risk injury to others, he is responsible for the consequences. Many of the contexts of individual provisions, which risk seeming meaningless or even faintly absurd to us, may thus have been selected not for their frequency or prominence at the time, but for the opportunity they provided of setting out a basic theoretical position, which would be understood to apply to many other contexts as well. It is in this sense, of starting the process of *thinking* about the law, and moving from the collective provisions of a kin-regulated society towards recognisable modern concepts of responsibility, trial and punishment, that Old English Laws probably had their strongest impact and may be said to stand at the head of a tradition that has continued unbroken (and unresolved) to the present.

---

[47] Including in some sense a master's responsibility for a slave? See for example Ethelbert ch.89, 90.

MANUSCRIPTS

BL Burney 277 f.42 – Ker 136, Liebermann Bu. Fragment of Alfred/Ine, of first half of 11th century, possibly of Kentish provenance.

BL Nero A.i ff/3–57 – Ker 163, Thorpe/Liebermann G. Alfred/Ine and other fragments. Middle 11th century. The collection begins with Cnut and works backwards, an order seemingly favoured in Anglo-Saxon times, and perhaps indicating their status in current law. This MS. was "made for ecclesiastical use at York or Worcester," (Richards 1986, p.177) and Part 2 of the MS. can be directly associated with Wulfstan.

BL Otho B.xi – Ker 180, Liebermann Ot. Old English Bede, WS genealogy, Chronicle, list of Popes/Bishops, Laws of Athelstan, Laws of Alfred, Burghal Hidage etc. Written first half of 11th century at Winchester. Perhaps a text drawn up by the clergy for the instruction of the laity (see Richards 1986, p.176).

CCCC173 ff.1–56 – Ker 39, Thorpe/Liebermann E. The Parker Chronicle and Laws. Laws of Alfred and Ine, written mid 10th century at Winchester, and transferred later to Canterbury possibly by Alfheah (Archbishop in 1006). The contents suggest this MS. was "a record of the achievements of the West-Saxon dynasty" (Richards 1986, p.173).

CCCC201 pt.B – Liebermann D. "A sprawling miscellany of Wulfstan's homilies, ecclesiastical institutes, and laws" re-copied in the mid 11th century. See Richards 1986, p.178. A text little regarded by Thorpe or Liebermann, but rescued from obscurity by Dorothy Whitelock.

CCCC383 – Ker 65, Thorpe/Liebermann B. Fragmentary collection of laws, some Alfred, Edward, Edmund, etc. and genealogies. Perhaps written at St Paul's, London, around 1100. Only source for Alfred-Guthrum and Edward-Guthrum. According to Richards (1986, p.183) "a plain book, seemingly intended as a reference work" that "implies Norman concern for governing people of disparate classes and nationalities and for learning English social custom."

Textus Roffensis (Maidstone, Kent Archives Office, MS. DRc/RI) – Ker 373, Thorpe/Liebermann H. A large-scale collection of laws (in part deriving from CCCC383?) plus genealogies, compiled for Bishop Ernulf (1115–1124). Only source for early Kentish Laws. Considered by Liebermann (1898) to be based on a compilation of ca. 1000 AD, perhaps from Canterbury, which would have already contained the Kentish Laws. Apparently written out as part of a concerted effort to codify law texts in reign of Henry I; or perhaps (since joined with a cartulary) as a statement of the position of Rochester with respect to local and national contexts; but also perhaps a personal commission by Bishop Ernulf, who as Abbot of Peterborough 1107–1114 likely encouraged the continuation of the Anglo-Saxon Chronicle there, and may have had a keen personal interest in English tradition.

INDIVIDUAL LAW-CODES

Note: the *Monumenta Germaniae Historica* series is abbreviated to *MGH*.

The Twelve Tablets – Rome, ca. 450 BC. An early general exposition of law, probably with Laws of Solon in Athens as a prototype. Punishments (corporal, capital and forfeiture of goods) undertaken in the name of specific gods.

Codex Theodosianus (Theodosius II – issued ca. 438). Collection of 'constitutiones' (ordinances) from Constantine onwards, in 16 books.

Justinian (Justinian I) published AD 519 the **Code** (*leges* or statute laws, from as far back as Hadrian's time), in AD 533 the **Institutes**, in AD 533 the **Digest** (a sort of encyclopaedia made of "excerpts from the writings of the jurists"); Code revised in AD 534, and subsequent **Novellae** (up-dates) issued. "They cover the whole field of law, public and private, civil and criminal, secular and ecclesiastical. It cannot be said that they afford pleasant reading: they are so disfigured by redundancy of language, involved periods and nauseous self-glorification. But it cannot be denied that many of those which deal with the private law embody reforms of great moment and of most salutary tendency." (Muirhead and Goudy). Possibly available in western Europe after Charlemagne's time.

Codex Euricanus or **Laws of Euric** (King of Vizigoths, 466–485) ca.476. Includes Christian and Roman-style provisions.

Edictum Theoderici – (Theoderic, king of the Ostrogoths) ca.500 AD. ed. K. Zeumer, *MGH Leges Nationum Germanicarum*, I. Leges Visigothorum; Hanover, 1902, pp.1–32). 155 chapters, mainly criminal law, drawing on Roman sources. (See Muirhead and Goudy)

Lex Romana Visigothorum or **Breviary of Alaric** (Alaric II, King of the Western Goths) ca.506 – ed. K. Zeumer, *MGH Leges Nationum Germanicarum, I. Leges Visigothorum*; Hanover, 1902, pp.37–456.

Compiled by a commission of lawyers appointed by the king, based especially on the Theodosian Code, for use in Spain. "The Breviary exercised great influence in western Europe; and there is no question that, until the rise of the Bologna school in the end of the eleventh century, it was from it more than from the books of Justinian that western Europe, other than Italy, acquired its scanty knowledge of Roman law." (Muirhead and Goudy)

Lex Burgundionum or **Lex Gundobada** 483x532 – ed. L. R. de Salis, *MGH Legum* Section 1, 2.1 (Hanover 1902). Contains theoretical prologue and some 105 chapters. Concise (Germanic) regulations about physical injuries, i.e. tariff of values, wergilds etc. Used also by Franks. ca.500 a **Lex Romana Burgundionum** was devised, to apply to Romans living under the Burgundians, but later replaced by the **Breviary of Alaric**.

Lex Salica ca.507–11. ed. K. A. Eckhardt (*MGH*, Legum, 5: 4,2, Hanover, 1969). General law-code based on the traditions of the Franks, with later recensions sanctioned by specific monarchs e.g. Pippin, Charlemagne. Some 98 chapters detailing offences and compensation. "A wholly pagan code." (Wallace-Hadrill, 1971, p.36).

Ethelbert of Kent ca.602–3. First law-code issued in England. Modelled on earlier Frankish, Gothic and Burgundian Laws, but in content local and customary (Witney p.93). Asserts status of Church and King, with many detailed laws esp. list of 'tarrifs' for injuries.

Hlothhere/Eadric of Kent 673x686, probably 685–6. Short general law-code, no tariff lists. References indicate a continuity with customary law processes, rather than centralised administration.

Wihtred of Kent 695–6. Short general code, marking the re-unification of Kent in the 690s after a period of uncertain rule. Lays emphasis on groups oaths (4 people) or the supporting oath of a lord in resolving disputes. "The code is in marked contrast to those of Æthelberht and of Hlothere, both in its preoccupation with ecclesiastical matters and because it introduces a sharply punitive element into a body of custom which had been based chiefly upon conceptions of restitution and the settlement of private wrongs" (Witney, 1982, p.165).

Ine of Wessex 688x694. Extended code with wide coverage, including (unusually) aspects of land ownership. Consulted by Alfred and only found in MSS as an appendix to his own law-code.

Differs from Kentish laws in providing for two classes of nobility (gesið), at 6 and 3 times the rate of a freeman, but with no semi-free (læt) class.

Offa of Mercia 757x796. Lost law-code, known to and consulted by Alfred who may have included some of its provisions in his own laws.

Alfred of Wessex 871x899, probably 880s. An extensive code, usually associated in MSS with the text of Ine's laws and referring internally also to Offa's and Ethelbert's law-codes. Preface considers biblical source of Law; laws themselves cover a wide range of situations, and provide a theoretical base for yet wider application.

Alfred and Guthrum. Treaty setting boundary between Wessex and Danelaw, and regulating trade and the risk of criminals fleeing to the Danelaw.

Edward of Wessex 899x925.

1 Edward: Directions to the king's *gerefan* (officers) on trade (especially witnessing of sales), ownership rights of bookland and folkland, perjury, etc. Enacts that a local court shall be held every month.

2 Edward: Short law-code, issued at Exeter and presumably supplementary to Alfred's. General enactments on use of sureties as defence in charge of theft, and common duty to track stolen cattle; also some innovations: a general oath of loyalty, confirmation that failure to pay compensation would lead to servile status, and denial of any right to transfer liege lord without permission.

Edward and Guthrum. Confirmation of Alfred **and** Guthrum, but establishing rights of Christian Church in Danelaw, and bringing Danelaw more into line with basic West Saxon Law.

Athelstan of England 925x939.

1 Athelstan: Ecclesiastical matters (tithes and Church dues). Possibly one code with 2 Athelstan.

2 Athelstan.: General code, issued at Greatanlea (Grately near Andover). Wide coverage e.g. theft, tithes, moneyers, ports, ordeals etc. Raises age of capital punishment for theft from 10 years old (Ine ch.7) to 12 years, unless an exacerbated offence. Ch.13–18 refer to boroughs e.g. trade only to be permitted within boroughs,

25

and provision for maintaining fortresses and army. Attempts to
tackle problem of instability by declaring anyone without the surety
of a liege lord or kin an outlaw; similarly, anyone who persistently
did not attend the local assembly could be fined or executed. Places
special emphasis on role of ordeal in settling a range of
accusations. Provides that royal reeves shall be supervised by
bishops.

3   Athelstan.: A letter or petition from the people of Kent indicating
their acceptance of 2 Athelstan, while suggesting some
modifications e.g. no freeman of good character to be refused
permission to change his liege lord, rich or noble offenders to be
transferred elsewhere in the kingdom. Survives only in Latin form
in *Quadripartitus*.

4   Athelstan.: Issued at Thundersfield (?near Reigate). Reconfirms 2
Athelstan while accepting some revision of its terms. All found
guilty (on ordeal) of theft, to be executed (rather than sold as slave
or ransomed?): a free man presumably to be hanged, a free woman
to be thrown off a cliff or drowned; a man slave to be stoned to
death by other slaves, a female slave to be burned to death.
Survives only in Latin form.

5   Athelstan.: Issued at Exeter. A tightening up of general provisions;
confirms limited 'outlawry' i.e. transfer to another area, and aims to
ensure justice by fining reeves who act corruptly.

6   Athelstan: Establishes (apparently for London and surrounding
area) tithings and hundreds as local provision for security and
compensation, with monthly hundred court. Raises the age for the
death penalty to 15; reaffirms the need for a general oath of loyalty,
to be administered by reeves.

Edmund of England 939x946

1   Edmund: ecclesiastical provisions (payment of tithes, celibacy of
monks).

2   Edmund: Secular provisions, especially designed to limit the extent
of a feud by insisting on the neutrality of kin. Only the perpetrator
can be liable to vengeance, though kin to participate in
compensation if they wish to. Details process for settling a case of
manslaughter: after agreement between killer and dead man's kin is
reached, the king's peace (*mund*) applies to both parties, and

payment is to be made at fixed instalments. No appeal to the king is allowed until all processes of local justice are exhausted.

3   Edmund: 'Apud Culintonam' (?Colyton, Devon). Short Latin code reinforcing some elements of Edward's and Athelstan's codes, and providing for a general oath of allegiance. New provision for slave committing theft to be hanged or flogged and scalped (presumably according to seriousness of offence).

Edgar of England 959x975

1   Edgar: The Hundred Ordinance, arguably belonging to Edmund's reign. Establishes local courts to meet every month.

2   Edgar: (Andover). Ecclesiastical provisions; probably one code with 3 Edgar.

3   Edgar: Short general (secular) code, with emphasis on safeguards against the misuse of the justice system.

4   Edgar: Issued at Wihtbordesstan. Possibly drafted by Archbishop Dunstan (see Whitelock *EHD*), and related by some to the plague of 962, but Wormald (1978) prefers 973 (Edgar's coronation year). The provisions have a more moral and universal tone: persistent failure to pay rent/tithes to lead to forfeiture of property and even life; such payments to be enforced by reeves. Everyone must have a place within a surety system; all transactions to be witnessed, all purchases of livestock to be declared, all journeys to be declared in advance. Within limits, the Danes are to establish their own best regulations. Technically a writ rather than a law-code.

Ethelred of England 979x1016

1   Ethelred, issued at Woodstock. General code, perhaps dating from 997. All freemen to provide surety (*borh*), failing which he may be investigated and if necessary executed by the king's reeve. Freemen and slaves alike liable to undergo the ordeal, and to execution on second offence.

2   Ethelred, a treaty with the Vikings (specifically Olaf). ca.991; expanded ca.1000.

3   Ethelred, issued at Wantage. Mostly concerned with the Danelaw and perhaps a companion code to 1 Ethelred ("designed as complementary pieces of legislation" Wormald, 1978,p.61). King's peace declared to apply to many public assemblies; emphasis on ordeal rather than oaths for deciding guilt. Outlawry to apply

everywhere i.e. no transfer system. Thane class made answerable only to the king himself.

4 Ethelred. Latin code, 'De Institutis Lundonie'. May include fragments of a lost law-code dating from 984–5 i.e. upon Ethelred's "assumption of personal power" (Wormald, 1978, p.63).

5 Ethelred, code of AD1008, issued at Enham. Drawn up by Wulfstan.

6 Ethelred, version of the previous, probably prepared for the Danelaw

7 Ethelred: (Bath). Edict aimed at coping with troubles following raids in 1008, mainly penitential in tone.

8 Ethelred: an ecclesiastical code, dated 1014. Defines a Christian king as Christ's deputy among a Christian people (ch.2).

9 Ethelred: fragment of a code issued at Woodstock. Perhaps related to Ethelred 8.

10 Ethelred: fragment of a code datable to 1009–16, perhaps part of Ethelred 5/6.

Cnut of England 1016–1035

1 Cnut: ecclesiastical concerns. Forms one code with 2 Cnut.

2 Cnut, Secular law-code, issued between 1020 and 1023; drawn up by Wulfstan. Extensive code, including a large percentage of earlier material.

Quadripartitus, ca.1114 AD. Latin version of laws. Named after its four constituent books: 1, Old English Laws in Latin; 2, state papers; books 3 and 4 now lost.

NOTES ON TERMINOLOGY

BT = Joseph Bosworth and J. Northcote Toller *An Anglo-Saxon Dictionary* (Oxford, 1898, with *Supplement*, 1921)

Lieb. = Liebermann, 1906.

M&G = Muirhead and Goudy, 1910–11

R = Richards 1989, pp.13–15

æ(w) 'law', 'proper observances' etc.

að 'an oath, a swearing' (BT)

gebetan 'to make better... make amends, reparation' (BT)

borg/borh 'a security, pledge, loan, bail... a person who gives security, a surety' (BT); 'Borg, Bürgenschaft' i.e. surety, loan, security, bail (Lieb.)

bot 'help, assistance, remedy, cure... compensation, recompense, reparation' (BT); 'Besserung, Busse, Strafe' i.e. reparation, atonement, penalty (Lieb.). Such payments might be made in kind as much as in money, and would be collected from among the kin of the offender (if necessary) and distributed among the kin in the case of compensation for death.

ceorl 'a peasant proprietor' (*EHD*); 'a freeman of the lowest class, churl' (BT); a free man as opposed to a 'þeow', a commoner as opposed to an 'eorl'.

dom 'judgement, judicial sentence, decree, ordinance, law' (BT)

ealdormon 'alderman, duke, nobleman of the highest rank... principal judicial officer of the shire...appointed by the king... earl' (BT)

eorl 'a nobleman'

esne 'man of the servile class, a servant, retainer, man, youth... a poor freeman' (BT); seemingly equivalent to 'slave' in Ethelbert's Laws, but less obviously so in Alfred's, where may equal 'hireling'.

feoh 'cattle, living animals... money, value... goods, property' (BT); especially movable goods.

folc-riht 'folkright, common law, public right, the understood compact by which every freeman enjoys his rights as a freeman' (BT); 'customary law'

frið-stow 'a peace-place, refuge, asylum' (BT)

gield 'a payment of money, recompense' (BT)

gieldan 'to yield, pay, render' (BT)

gylt – 'offence' (thus Ine, Alfred); 'guilt, sin' etc.

lagu 'law, statue, decree' (BT); 'law'; Viking (Norse) equivalent of Old English *æw*; first used in Edgar's code in the context of the Danelaw; *dom/aew* cede to *lagu* in Wulfstan's time (see Richards 1989 p.16)

magas 'kinfolk' – the extended family group typical of Anglo-Saxon society, with property held communally and each member responsible for the others.

morgen-gifu 'morning-gift'; 'the gift made by the husband to the wife on the morning after the consummation of the marriage' (BT, *EHD*)

mund 'Schutz, Zuflucht' i.e. 'protection, refuge' (Lieb.); 'protection, guardianship extended by the king to the subject, 'the king's peace', by the head of a family to its members' (BT); literally protection offered by hand, and so personal in source; used especially of the king's direct protection, extending to all or a particular subject, and so making assaults breaches of the king's peace. cf. Latin 'manus': "the power (hand) of a husband over his wife 'in familia', was originally the generic term for all the rights exercised, not only over the things belonging but also over the persons subject to the head of the house." (M&G)

mund-byrd 'protection, patronage, aid' (BT); right of giving protection (*EHD*); guarantee of personal protection; can be equivalent to 'mund'

nied/nead 'compulsion, force'; by Wulfstan's time can imply external necessity i.e. involuntary action.

ordal – 'ordeal' (1st used in 2 Athelstan)

riht 'right, law, what is just or proper, a right' etc. (BT); customary or traditional law.

sceat 'property, goods, wealth, treasure... money.... a coin, one twentieth of a shilling' (BT) – see also *scilling*

scilling 'shilling'. In Ethelbert's Kent, a gold coin, equivalent to the Frankish *tremissis*, and weighing 20 Troy grains. A *sceat* was a twentieth of this or 1 Troy Grain. But in Alfred's Wessex a shilling was a silver coin, half the value of a Kentish shilling, and equivalent to 5 silver pennies. After Witney (1982, p.94) a table of equivalents can be deduced for Kent: 1 ox = 6 sheep; 1 eorl = 100 oxen or 300 shillings; 1 freeman = 100 shillings or 200 sheep; a *læt* or semi-free man might be worth 80, 120 or 160 sheep.

synne 'sin, offence, guilt'

tihtan/tihtlian/teon 'to accuse'

tun 'enclosure, homestead, a village, estate' etc. (BT)

þeow 'slave' (by birth, capture, debt or other legal process)

wed(d) 'a pledge, what is given as security... a solemn promise, compact' (BT); can also be used for the betrothal payment: "There were two parts to a marriage: the 'wedding', that is, the pledging or betrothal, when the bride-price was paid and the terms were agreed on; and the 'gift', the bridal itself, when the bride was given to the bridegroom, with feasting or ceremony. Ecclesiastical blessing was not necessary to the legality of the marriage, though the Church advocated it." (Whitelock, 1952, pp.152).

wergeld a person's value according to status, and from which compensation was worked out. "Wergeld, in its purest form [was] the blood-price, the sum paid in just compensation for a slaying" (Loyn, 1992, p.55).

wite 'punishment... fine' (BT) especially that money paid to the king or his officers as opposed to compensation.

Note on Conventions in Text

In the following translations, Old English (OE) original terms are specified in ornamental type in brackets, additions and explanations are in italic.

ÆTHELBERHT OF KENT

Introduction

The law-code of Ethelbert of Kent is the first attempt to bring a Romano-Christian tradition of written law to the English people, in line with the sort of codes operating among christianised nations on the continent (Ethelbert had married a Merovingian princess). The immediate model was thus the law of the Franks, and indeed Kent may have been subject not just to Frankish influence but even Frankish control or overlordship at this time.[1]

But while precedents for individual items in Ethelbert's Laws are possible in codes like the Lex Salica, so complicated are the interrelations in the continental codes that it becomes "well-nigh impossible to tell who is borrowing from whom".[2] Yet it is these later models rather any original Roman law that Bede surely had in mind when he says that Ethelbert made his laws "iuxta exempla Romanorum"[3] – rather than any direct imitation of Justinian, for example. In his modest way, the Kentish king seemed to be demonstrating "practical knowledge of Frankish government... to enhance his own royal authority",[4] and appropriately the code opens with matters of status, the compensation due Church, king, nobleman and commoner. General criminal legislation fills chapter 17–32, and thereafter follows a detailed tariff of compensation liable for injury, ordered approximately from hair down to toe...

---

[1] See Wallace-Hadrill (1971) p.25.
[2] ibid. p.38.
[3] *Historia Ecclesiastica* Bk.2 ch.5.
[4] Yorke (1990) p.41.

These are the regulations (domas) that Ethelbert the king promulgated in Augustine's lifetime.

1. God's property (feoh) and the Church's *if stolen*, compensate (gylde) twelve-fold. A bishop's property, compensate eleven-fold. A priest's property, compensate nine-fold. A deacon's property, compensate six-fold. A clerk's property, compensate three-fold. Breach of sanctuary (ciric-friþ), compensate two-fold. Breach of the peace of an Assembly (mæthl-frið), compensate two-fold.[5]

2. If the king summons his people (leode)[6] to him and anyone does injury (yfel) to them there, a double compensation (bote) and fifty shillings *fine* to the king.

3. If the king is drinking *i.e. is resident* at someone's home, and anyone commits some sort of offence (lyswæs hwæt) there, he shall pay two-fold compensation (gebete).

4. If a freeman steal from the king, he shall pay back (forgylde) ninefold compensation (gylde).

5. If someone kills another man on the king's premises (tun), he shall pay in compensation (gebete) 50 shillings.

6. If anyone kills a freeman, 50 shillings shall be due the king as a sum for the loss of a subject (drihtin-beage).[7]

---

[5] In the last two cases, the violence presumably carries a penalty in itself, which is doubled if committed on Church property or in the context of an official 'Council' meeting.

[6] Attenborough compares 'leod' to Frankish 'leudes' and renders it 'lieges', presumably those who owe a special duty of advice. Witney (1982, p.96) renders it as "the king's armed followers." The nature of the assembly involved is unspecified, however.

[7] This makes manslaughter a royal concern, because of the duties linking king and subject, and thus a fine is payable to the king, presumably on top of any other penalty (e.g. as in ch.20). Whitelock in *EHD* takes 'drihtinbeage' as a payment made in rings.

7. If anyone kills the king's own smith (ambiht-smiđ) or guide (laad-rincmannan),[8] he shall pay a proper compensation (meduman leod-gelde forgelde).[9]

8. *For breach of the* king's personal protection (mund-byrd),[10] *a fine of* fifty shillings.

9. If a freeman (frig-man) steals from another freeman, he shall pay compensation (gebete) threefold, and the king shall take the fine (wite) and all the [stolen] goods (æhtan).[11]

10. If someone lies with one of the king's female slaves (mægden-man), he shall pay as compensation (gebete) 50 shillings.

11. If she is a *corn*-grinding slave (grindende þeowa), he shall pay as compensation (gebete) 25 shillings. *If she be of* the third *rank*, 12 shillings.

12. *For killing* a tenant (fedesl)[12] of the king, 20 shillings shall be paid over (forgelde).

13. If someone slays a man on a nobleman's premises (on eorles tune), he shall pay as compensation (gebete) 12 shillings.

14. If someone lies with a nobleman's serving-maid (eorles birele), he shall pay in compensation (gebete) 20 shillings.

15. *For breach of* a freeman's personal protection (ceorles mund-byrd), 6 shillings.

---

8 Laadrincmann – 'messenger' (Atten, *EHD*), 'conductor, escort' (CHM), "more a herald" (Witney, 1982, p.98).

9 Leodgelde – in addition to any wergeld (Atten) or a freeman's rate although these were non-free servants (Lieb)? Or a special use of 'leod' implying status? (cf. ch.2 above)

10 On this term, see 'mundbyrd' in separate list.

11 These provisions seem drastic, if one translates 'all the man's goods' (Atten.); perhaps the penalties are alternatives (Lieb.), or, as here translated, the disputed goods alone are intended. The king's 'fine' might be a proportion of the increased compensation?

12 Fedesl: 'Koenigskostgaenger' (Lieb) i.e. boarder or renter; cf. 'famuli qui regio pastu utebantur' (Ethelweard's Chronicle 878).

16. If someone lies with a freeman's serving-maid (ceorles birelan), he shall pay as compensation (gebete) 6 shillings. If with a slave-woman (ðeowan) of the second *rank*, 50 sceattas. If *with one* of the third *rank*, 30 sceattas.

17. If someone is first to force his way (ge-irneþ) into someone else's premises (tun), he shall pay as compensation (gebete) 6 shillings; he that enters next *shall pay* 3 shillings; each *that enters* subsequently, a shilling.

18. If someone supplies another with weapons, when a dispute (ceas[t]) is happening, though no one commits any injury (yfel), still he shall pay as compensation (gebete) 6 shillings.

19. If highway robbery (weg-reaf) is committed *with such weapons*, he *i.e. the provider of any weapon* shall pay as compensation (gebete) 6 shillings.

20. If anyone kills another man *with such weapons*, he *i.e. the provider* shall pay as compensation (gebete) 20 shillings.[13]

21. If someone slays (of-slæhð) another man, he shall pay (gebete) a proper compensation (medume leod-geld) of 100 shillings.

22. If someone slays another man, he shall pay over (forgelde) 20 shillings at the open grave,[14] and the whole wergeld (leod) within 40 days.

23. If a killer (bana) escapes (gewiteþ) from the country (of lande), the kinsfolk (magas) shall pay over (forgelden) half the wergeld (leod).

24. If anyone puts bonds (gebindeþ, *as restoration of text*) on a freeman, he shall pay as compensation (gebete) 20 shillings.[15]

---

[13] This may mean during the course of a highway robbery (as in ch.19), or in any circumstance.

[14] At the open grave i.e. before the victim's burial has taken place. Is the implication that the victim's kin might otherwise wish to vow revenge over the body itself? Witney (1982, pp.94–5, cf. p.167) feels this might be a sort of deposit at this stage, a 'heals-fang', that is the "first instalment of the wergeld, representing one fifth of the whole."

[15] The implication is, if someone treats a freeman as a slave.

25. If someone kills a freeman's dependent (ceorlæs hlaf-ætan), he shall pay compensation (gebete) of 6 shillings.[16]

26. If anyone slays a semi-slave (læt),[17] he shall pay over (forgelde) 80 shillings for one of best *rank*; if of second *rank*, he shall pay over 60 shillings; *if* of third *rank*, he shall pay over 40 shillings.

27. If a freeman (fri-man) commits criminal trespass (edor-brecþe),[18] he shall pay as compensation (gebete) 6 shillings.

28. If someone seizes goods (feoh) when inside, he *i.e. the intruder* shall pay (gebete) threefold compensation (gelde).

29. If a freeman improperly enters such an enclosure (edor geganged), he shall pay in compensation (gebete) 4 shillings.

30. If someone slays another man, he shall pay (gelde) with his own money (scætte) or goods (feo), which, of whatever sort they be, must be undamaged/unblemished (unfacne).[19]

---

[16] Presumably in addition to any other penalty; this compensation would be due the freeman as master, cf. ch.6 above.

[17] A 'læt', perhaps copied from continental laws, implies a class of person slightly below that of freeman e.g. a freed slave, or perhaps a non-Anglo-Saxon.

[18] Edorbrecþ is literally 'breach of enclosure or boundary' i.e. damage to or trespass on clearly marked property (perhaps including home or other buildings), presumably with the purpose of theft of livestock or goods. There is a duty on the owner to fence off private land in Ine ch.40, 42, which may indicate a distinction between communal (kin) ownership and private ownership, the latter (as the more recent development) being specially dealt with in these laws? Alternately, edor may imply an earlier, semi-mystical boundary: the Germanic *Indiculus Superstitionum* ch.23 complains 'De sulcis circa villas' – of furrows cut round villages, with presumably a magical or ritual intent.

[19] Clearly, in a farming-based society, however sophisticated, money is not the basis of everyday transactions, but is used in the Laws here as a standard of value. Compensation is likelier to be in the form of livestock, agricultural produce or particular items of manufactured value. The insistence that these be perfect is of course reasonable, but also has ritualistic tone?

31. If one freeman (fri-man) lies with another freeman's wife, he shall render (abiege) the wergeld,[20] and procure with his own money a second wife *for the man* and bring her to his house.

32. If someone breaks through (þurh-sti[g]ð) the perimeter of a homestead (riht-ham-scyld),[21] let him pay (forgelde) according to its value.

33. If seizing *or pulling* by the hair (feax-fang)[22] takes place, 50 sceattas as compensation (to bote).

34. If the exposure (blice) of bone occurs, *the aggressor* shall pay as compensation (gebete) 3 shillings.

35. If the cutting (bite) of a bone occurs, *the aggressor* shall pay as compensation (gebete) 4 shillings.

36. If the outer part of the skull (hion) gets broken, *the aggressor* shall pay in compensation (gebete) 10 shillings.

37. If both *outer and inner* are *broken*, *the aggressor* shall pay in compensation (gebete) 20 shillings.

38. If a shoulder is disabled, *the aggressor* shall pay in compensation (gebete) 30 shillings.

39. If either ear *is deprived* of all hearing, *the aggressor* shall pay in compensation (gebete) 25 shillings.

40. If an ear is cut off, *the aggressor* shall pay in compensation (gebete) 12 shillings.

41. If an ear is pierced (þirel), *the aggressor* shall pay in compensation (gebete) 3 shillings.[23]

---

[20] It is uncertain whose wergeld is payable – the offender's, the wife's, or the husband's.

[21] It is unclear how this varies from ch.27. See note 18 above.

[22] The act is, of course, one of humiliation within a cultural tradition – cf. ch.73 below. The Franks laid special emphasis on the status of hair length – see Wallace-Hadrill (1971) pp.17–18.

[23] In the later Laws of Alfred (Pref.11) this is a sign of enslavement. Most of the regulations here imply sword or dagger fighting (piercing implying a jab

42. If an ear is slashed (sceard), *the aggressor* shall pay in compensation (gebete) 6 shillings.

43. If an eye is put out, *the aggressor* shall pay in compensation (gebete) 50 shillings.

44. If mouth or eye become disfigured, *the aggressor* shall pay in compensation (gebete) 12 shillings.

45. If the nose is pierced (ðyrel), *the aggressor* shall pay in compensation (gebete) 9 shillings.

46. If one cheek is *pierced, the aggressor* shall pay in compensation (gebete) 3 shillings.

47. If both *cheeks* are pierced, *the aggressor* shall pay in compensation (gebete) 6 shillings.

48. If the nose is slashed (sceard) in some other way,[24] *the aggressor* shall pay in compensation (gebete) 6 shillings for each *cut*.

49. If it[25] is pierced, *the aggressor* shall pay in compensation (gebete) 6 shillings.

50. He that smashes (forslæhð) a chin bone shall pay over (forgelde) 20 shillings.

51. For any of the four front teeth, 6 shillings *shall be paid*. For a tooth that stands next to these, 4 shillings. For one that stands next to that, 3 shillings. And beyond that, a shilling for each tooth.

52. If the power of speech is removed (awyrd), 12 shillings. If the collarbone is broken, *the aggressor* shall pay in compensation (gebete) 6 shillings.

53. He who pierces an arm shall pay in compensation (gebete) 6 shillings. If the arm is broken, *the aggressor* shall pay in compensation (gebete) 6 shillings.

---

with the point of a knife, slash a sideways cut), but some may also have connotations of humiliation.

[24] Presumably other than by piercing.

[25] Something has been omitted here, as the piercing of a nose has already been mentioned (ch.45). Lieb suggests 'throat'.

54. If a thumb is cut off, 20 shillings. If a thumbnail is knocked off, *the aggressor* shall pay in compensation (gebete) 3 shillings. If someone strikes off a forefinger (scyte-finger), *the aggressor* shall pay in compensation (gebete) 9 shillings. If someone strikes off a middlefinger, *the aggressor* shall pay in compensation (gebete) 4 shillings. If someone strikes off a ring finger (gold-finger), *the aggressor* shall pay in compensation (gebete) 6 shillings. If someone strikes off a little finger, *the aggressor* shall pay in compensation (gebete) 11 shillings.[26]

55. For each fingernail, a shilling.

56. For a slight disfigurement (lærestan wlite-wamme), 3 shillings; for a more marked one, 6 shillings.

57. If someone strikes another on the nose with his fist, 3 shillings.

58. If there is a mark *or bruise* (dynt), one shilling. If he (i.e. the victim) takes the blow with his raised hand, *the aggressor* shall pay over (forgelde) one shilling.[27]

59. If the bruise (dynt) is black *and shows* outside the clothing, *the aggressor* shall pay in compensation (gebete) 30 sceattas.[28]

60. If *the bruise* be under the clothes, *the aggressor* shall pay in compensation (gebete) 20 sceattas for each *mark*.

61. If a belly-wound (hrif-wund) is sustained, *the aggressor* shall pay in compensation (gebete) 20 shillings. If it be punctured (þurh-ðirel), *the aggressor* shall pay in compensation (gebete) 20 shillings.

---

[26] The 'hierarchy' of fingers seems unusual: without thumb, nothing can be properly grasped, so its high value is expected. But the little finger plays no such clearly vital role. There may be a clue in the later (3 Edmund 4) provision that a thief should have his little finger cut short, so that this sort of damage might be especially demeaning. But with only one MS of the text, some error cannot be ruled out.

[27] i.e. even a blow warded off is to be compensated.

[28] i.e. in addition?

62. If the man needs medical attention (gegemed weorđeþ), *the aggressor* shall pay in compensation (gebete) 30 shillings.

63. If the man is wounded *in a way that causes* special concern (cearwund sie),[29] *the aggressor* shall pay in compensation (gebete) 30 shillings.

64. If anyone destroys the generative organ (gekyndelice lim), *the aggressor* shall pay three times the wergeld (leud-geldum). If he perforates (þurh-stin[g]đ) it, he shall pay in compensation (gebete) 6 shillings. If he part pierces it, he shall pay in compensation (gebete) 6 shillings.

65. If the thigh is broken, *the aggressor* shall pay in compensation (gebete) 12 shillings. If he becomes lame (healt), friends should (motan) arrange a settlement (seman).[30]

66. If a rib is broken in (forbrocen), *the aggressor* shall pay in compensation (gebete) 3 shillings.

67. If someone stabs through the thigh, 6 shillings *shall be paid* for each cut (stice). If *a stab is* over an inch *deep*, one shilling; *if* two inches *deep*, two *shillings*; over three *inches deep*, three shillings.

68. If the muscle of the thigh (wælt) is wounded, *the aggressor* shall pay in compensation (gebete) 3 shillings.

69. If a foot is *struck* off, *the aggressor* shall pay over (forgelde) 50 shillings.

70. If the big toe is *struck* off, *the aggressor* shall pay over (forgelde) 10 shillings.

71. For *loss of* any of the other toes, *the aggressor* shall pay (gelde) half as much as is quoted *for the respective fingers*.

---

[29] Cearwund is of uncertain meaning; following on from ch.62, it suggests a wound of the sort that needs special attention. BT Sup. suggest emendation to scearwund – a torn or jagged wound.

[30] Implying a sort of arbitration, as cases might vary very much.

72. If the nail of the big toe is *knocked* off, 30 sceattas in compensation (to bote). For each of the others, *the aggressor* shall pay in compensation (gebete) 10 sceattas.

73. If a freeborn woman (fri-wif), with long hair (loc-bore) commits any misconduct (leswæs hwæt), she shall pay in compensation (gebete) 30 shillings.[31]

74. Compensation to an unmarried woman (mægþ-bot) shall be *paid at the same rate* as for a freeman (friges mannes).

75. *For infringement of* the guardianship[32] (mund) of the best *rank* of nobly-born (eorl-cundre) widow, *the offender* shall pay as compensation (gebete) 50 shillings. *For a widow of the* second *rank*, 20 shillings; *for a widow of* the third *rank*, 12 shillings; *for a widow* of the fourth rank 6 shillings.

76. If someone abducts (genimeþ) a widow not his own *to control* (unagne), let the compensation (gelde) be twice the 'mund'.

77. If someone pays for (gebigeđ) a maid *as wife*, let the transaction be honoured (ceapi geceapod sy) if there is no deceit. If there is deception (facne), let him take her back to her home, and they shall return his money (scæt) to him.

78. If she bears a living child, she shall have half the money (scæt),[33] if the husband (ceorl) dies first.

79. If *she* wishes to leave[34] (bugan) with the children, she shall have half the money (scæt).

80. If the husband (ceorl) wishes to keep *the children, the wife shall have the same portion* as a child.

---

[31] Sexual misconduct is probably implied.

[32] Guardianship implying control of her property rights or her value in event of re-marriage?

[33] Here and in 79 and 81 Whitelock in *EHD* slightly changes the emphasis by translating 'sceat' as 'goods' i.e. half their communal possessions rather half of her original bride-price.

[34] Just as there is no formal marriage service until the Reformation, so here the concept of divorce is viewed from a practical rather than a religious one.

81. If she does not bear a child, her father's kin (fædering-magas) shall have the money (fioh) and the wedding-gift (morgen-gyfe).

82. If someone abducts (genimeþ) a maid (mægþ-mon) by force, *he shall pay* 50 shillings to her controller (agende), and after that purchase (ætgebicge) the consent of the controller *to the marriage*.

83. If she *i.e. the girl abducted* is promised (bewyddod) to another, and money has changed hands (in sceat), *the offender* shall pay in compensation (gebete) 20 shillings *to the intended bridegroom*.

84. If restitution (gæn-gang) *of the girl* is made, 35 shillings *compensation shall be paid*, and 15 shillings to the king.

85. If someone lies with the wife (cwynan) of a slave (esnes), while the husband (ceorle) is alive, *the offender* shall pay (gebete) a twofold compensation.

86. If one slave (esne) kills (ofslea) another *who is* guiltless (unsynningne), he shall pay over (forgelde) his whole value (weorð).[35]

87. If the eye and foot of a slave (esnes) be struck off, *the offender* shall pay him at full value.

88. If someone puts bonds on another man's slave (esne), *the offender* shall pay in compensation (gebete) 6 shillings.

89. *The penalty for* highway robbery (weg-reaf) against a slave (ðeowæs)[36] shall be three shillings.

90. If a slave (þeo) steals, *?the owner* shall pay compensation at twice the value *of the stolen goods*.

---

[35] Note that weorð is used here, for value of an object, not any word denoting wergeld.

[36] Note: Whitelock in *EHD* queries whether this may be highway robbery by a slave, but the compensation seems rather low for that?

ALFRED

The Preface or Introduction to these Laws is based entirely on biblical material, especially Mosaic Law.[1] The intention of this was clearly to associate the concept of human law with that of divine law, and to trace the descent of divine authority from its Old Testament form, through New Testament confirmation, into ecclesiastical canons and so to secular law in Alfred's present. The quotations from the Bible were selected and edited, either (as in the conclusion) to support an argument, or as in the body of the Introduction to present a manageable amount of material in a relevant form; but it is not simply a question of choosing those provisions that could be paralleled in ninth century conditions, for points of theoretical interest were also admissible that could be applied in broader circumstances. In total they read (inevitably) rather like a set of proverbs.[2]

---

[1] Liebermann (1916) vol.3 p.34 notes that the Bible had been previously invoked in law-codes, though not, I believe, to this extent. Whether the Vulgate Bible was used or the Vetus Latina (a collective name for pre-Jerome translations into Latin) cannot easily be determined; if the latter, then a possible connection with Asser may be suggested (see Dammery, 1990, vol.1, p.222 fn.). Yet Liebermann (vol.3 p.34) notes that the translation of Exodus 21:33 in this Preface ch.22 differs from that used in Alfred's Pastoral Care (ed. Sweet, p.459), so the biblical material is little aid to identifying a compiler. Liebermann (vol.3 p.37) also notes several apparent errors, on which see notes to ch.25, 37 and 40 below.

[2] There is indeed a set of proverbs attributed to Alfred in Middle English (edited by O. S. Arngart as *The Proverbs of Alfred* (Lund, 2 vols., 1942, 1955)). These poems take almost the form of a law-code i.e. are said to be promulgated by Alfred at a session of the Witan at Seaford (close to Dene in Sussex, where Asser was first introduced to Alfred); nonetheless the setting and the attribution of authorship are deemed fictional. The law-like tone of some of the text may come from its apparent dependence on a pseudo-Wulfstan homily which in turn echoed laws of Ethelred (see Arngart, 2, pp.6–7). Possible resemblances to Alfred's laws come in Proverb 2 which

43

Alfred's Introduction ch.1–10 are based on Exodus ch.20 (the Decalogue), his ch.11–23 on Exodus ch.21, his ch.24–30 on Exodus ch.22, and his ch.40–48 on Exodus ch.23 (chapters 21–23 of Exodus are known as 'The Book of the Covenant' and had a recognised unity). In the present translation, material in the Preface between ch.1 and 48 which is *not* explicitly derived from the Bible is <u>underlined</u>. (Such alterations have an important bearing on the discussion of whether material of this sort was included for merely theoretical/decorative effect, or was intended to be practical.)

Preface

The Lord was speaking these words to Moses, and said thus: "I am the Lord your God. I brought you out of the land of the Egyptians and from their bondage:

1. Do not love other strange gods above me.

2. [3] Do not speak My name idly, for you will not be guiltless with Me if you idly speak My name.

3. Remember to hallow the rest-day. Work for yourselves six days, and on the seventh rest yourselves. For in six days <u>Christ</u>[4] made the heavens and the earth, the seas and all creatures that are in them,

---

links obedience to a lord with honour to God (cf. Alfred, Introduction 37); Proverb 4 which exhorts clerk and knight to even-handed justice (cf. Int.43); the same Proverb, which warns that each shall reap as he sow, and that judgement comes home to one's own door (cf. Int.49); and Proverb 26 which warns against confiding in foolish people (cf. Int.40–41).

[3] The second commandment, do not make graven images and worship them, is omitted here, and put in later (as ch.10) in alternative form. This may have come about from respect for the provisions of the Council of Nicaea in 787, which approved the veneration of image and relics. (This was an embarrassment when 16th century Protestants sought precedent for their interpretation of religion in this particular section of the Anglo-Saxon record.)

[4] Christ here is used as synonymous with God the Father, as is commonly the case in OE texts, suggesting emphasis on the unity rather than the diversity of the Trinity.

and rested himself on the seventh day, and therefore God has sanctified it.

4. Honour your father and your mother that God gave you so that you may be the longer living on earth.

5. Do not kill (sleah).

6. Do not lie *in sexual union* secretly.

7. Do not steal.

8. Do not speak false evidence.

9. Do not wish for your neighbour's property (ierfes) unrightfully.

10. Do not make yourselves golden or silver gods.[5]

11. These are the regulations (domas) that you should set for them. If anyone buy (gebicgge) a <u>Christian</u> slave (þeow),[6] let him serve for six years *and* on the seventh let him be free without payment (orceapunga). With such clothes as he entered into *service,* let him leave with. If he has a wife of his own *providing,* let her leave with him. If the master (hlaford) provided him with a wife, both she and her children shall belong to the master. If the slave then says "I do not want *to leave* my master or my wife or my child <u>or my property</u> (ierfe)",[7] let his master bring him to the door of the Temple (temples) and perforate his ear with an awl as a sign that he shall ever afterwards be a slave.

12. Though someone sell (bebycgge) his daughter into slavery (þeowenne) do not let her be <u>a slave</u> entirely as are other <u>maid servants</u> (mennenu).[8] He has not the right to sell her abroad among

---

5 See note to ch.1, above. The second commandment (Exodus 20:4–5) is omitted, and this version supplied from 20:23.

6 The Bible refers to a 'Hebrew' not a Christian slave; while the change is in keeping with the spirit of the original it presumably meant this provision need not apply to a captive Viking (for instance).

7 The additional reference could be to property as land or house or possessions, clarifying that such (provided no doubt by the master) did not become the slave's on manumission.

8 The Bible here has the slightly obscure "she shall not go out as the men servants do", which seems to imply a servile status without later release

foreign people.[9] But if he who bought her does not care (recce) for her, let her be free among a foreign (elþeodig) people. But if he *i.e. the purchaser* allows his son to cohabit (hæmanne) with her, <u>give her the *morning* gift (gyfta) and ensure that she has clothing and that she has the value of her maidenhood, that is the dowry (weotuma) – let him give her that</u>.[10] If he does none of those things for her, then she shall be free.

13. The person who slays (ofslea) another deliberately (his gewealdes), shall suffer death.[11] He that has killed another <u>in self defence (nedes) or involuntarily (unwillum) or unintentionally (unwealdum)</u>, as God delivered him *i.e. the 'victim'* into his hands, and *providing* he *i.e. the killer* did not set a trap (ymbsyrede) for him – *in that case* let him be worthy of his life, <u>and of *settling by* customary compensation</u>[12] (folcryhtre bote), if he should seek asylum (friðstowe). If however anyone deliberately (of giernesse) and intentionally (gewealdes) kill his neighbour treacherously (þurh searwa), pluck (aluc) him from my altar so that he should suffer death.[13]

14. He that attacks (slea) his father or his mother shall suffer death.

(meaningless to a dependent woman?). On not selling abroad, which is in the source, though taken out of order here, compare Preface ch.15 below.

9 The provision against selling a slave abroad echoes Ine ch.11, and is in contrast to Wihtred ch.26 where selling abroad is a specific penalty.

10 The Bible simply says "he shall deal with her after the manner of daughters."

11 The tautological 'swelte se deaðe' represents the Biblical 'morte moriatur'.

12 The Bible provides only for flight to some refuge.

13 An important distinction is made here between 'fair' and 'unfair' killing, partly on the basis of motivation, partly on that of method of killing (e.g. a secret attack implies plan and premeditation – in later Saga accounts it was important whether the killing was openly acknowledged or kept secret). A similar distinction between murder and (involuntary) manslaughter remains with us. In the lesser case, the 'killer' had the right to make a financial settlement, but in the case of murder, no right of sanctuary or settlement by payment was allowed.

15. He that abducts (forstæle) a freeman (frione) and sells (bebycgge) him,[14] and it is proved (onbestæled) so that he cannot absolve (bereccan) himself, let him suffer death. He that curses (werge) his father or his mother, let him suffer death.

16. If someone attacks (slea) his neighbour with a stone or with *his* fist, but he *i.e. the victim* can still get about (gangan) with *the aid of* a staff, let him *i.e. the aggressor* provide him with a doctor (læce) and do his *i.e. the victim's* work *for him* for as long as he *i.e. the victim* cannot himself.

17. He that attacks (slea) his own non-free servant (þeowne esne) or his maidservant (mennen), and they are not dead *as a result of the attack* but live two or three days, he *i.e. the aggressor* shall not be so entirely guilty (scyldig), because it was his own property *he damaged.* But if *the slave* be dead the same day, then the guilt rests on him *i.e. the aggressor.*[15]

18. If anyone in *the course of a* dispute (on ceare) injure (gewerde) a pregnant woman (eacniend-wif), let him make compensation (bete) for the hurt <u>as judges</u> (domeras)[16] decide in his case (him gereccan). If she be dead, let him give life for life (selle sawle wið sawle).[17]

---

[14] The creation of slaves by capture in raids or because of indebtedness and subsequent sale abroad was a worrying feature throughout this period, most clearly enunciated in Wulfstan's early 11th Century 'Sermo Lupi'. cf. note 9 above.

[15] The point of this seems to be that a master has the right to punish a slave severely, and if that punishment leads to the slave's death, unintentionally, no great offence has been committed. But murder of a slave is as serious as any other murder.

[16] In the Bible, a penalty depending on the demand of the husband.

[17] This and ch.19 following are the only obvious references to 'talionic' measures i.e. retribution in kind – 'an eye for an eye' and so on, a feature of Mosaic and early Roman Law. In general, the death penalty is related in Alfred's Laws to the moral seriousness of the crime, not the fact that the loss of one life is being repaid with the loss of another.

19. If anyone put out (oþ-do) another's eye, let him give (selle) his own *for it.* Tooth for tooth. Hand for hand. Foot for foot. Burn (bærning) for burn. Wound for wound. Bruise (læl) for bruise.

20. If anyone strike the eye of his slave (þeowe) or maidservant (þeowenne) out and so makes them one-eyed, let him free (ge-orfreoge) them for that. If he strike out a tooth, let him do the same.

21. If an ox gore a man or woman (wer oþþe wif) so that they are dead, let it be stoned to death (mid stanum ofworpod) and do not let the flesh be eaten. The owner (hlaford) shall not be liable (bið unscyldig) if the ox was butting (hnitol) two days before that or even three, and the owner did not know of it. But if he knew of it and would not shut (betynan) it *i.e. the animal* in, and then it killed (ofsloge) a man or woman, let it be stoned to death and let the master be killed (ofslegen) or made to pay (forgolden) as the Witan consider proper (to rihte finden). If it gore (ofstinge) a son or daughter, let the same penalty apply (þæs ilcan domes sie he wyrðe). But if it gore (ofstinge) a slave or serving-woman (þeow-mennen), let the owner give (geselle) 30 shillings of silver and let the ox be stoned to death.

22. If anyone dig a well (wæter-pyt) or open up (ontyne) a closed one and does not close it up again, let him pay (gelde) for whatever cattle (neat) fall in; *but* let him have the dead *animal* for his own use.

23. If an ox wound another man's ox *so* it is dead, let them sell (bebycggen) the *live* ox and share the proceeds (weorð), and also the flesh of the dead *ox.* But if the owner knew the ox was butting and would not restrain (healdan) it, let him hand over (selle) the other *i.e. live* ox for it *but* let him have all the flesh *of the dead ox* for his own use.

24. If anyone steal (forstele) another man's ox and kill (ofslea) or sell (bebycgge) it, let him give two[18] *oxen* in restitution. And four sheep for one *stolen.* If he *i.e. the thief* does not have anything to give *in*

---

[18] In the Vulgate five oxen in restitution.

restitution, let him be sold (beboht) himself *to raise* the money (fio).[19]

25. If a thief break into a man's house by night and is killed (ofslegen) there, he *i.e. the house-owner* shall not be guilty of manslaughter (mansleges scyldig). But if he *i.e. the house-owner* does this after sunrise, he is guilty of manslaughter, and shall himself perish (swelte), <u>unless he acted in self-defence</u> (nied-dæda wære). If there is found in the possession of the living[20] *thief* things he had already stolen, let him make restitution (forgielde) for it two-fold.

26. If anyone damage (gewerde) another man's vineyard or his crops (æcras) or any part of his estate (landes), let him pay compensation (gebete) according to how it is assessed (swa hit mon ge-eahtige).

27. If a fire is lit (ontended) in order to burn rubbish (ryt),[21] let him who started (ontent) the fire pay compensation (gebete) for any *consequent* damage (æf-werdelsan).

28. If anyone entrusts (oþ-fæste) any possession (fioh) to his friend and *the friend* appropriates (stæle) it for himself,[22] let him *i.e. the friend* clear himself *and prove* that he committed no fraud (facn) in the matter. If it was livestock (cucu feoh), and he says that raiders

---

[19] This provision (which in the Bible follows the provision about house-breaking which is ch.25 here) outlines what may have been quite a common outcome of a law case: if the accused could not make restitution, he was himself liable to be sold into slavery – whether temporarily (as implied by ch.16 above) or permanently perhaps depending on the sum to be raised? See my introduction, note 45.

[20] In the Latin 'living' applies to animals in the thief's possession rather than the thief himself.

[21] BT Supplement suggest that 'ry(h)t' is the sort of scrub found on rough land; if so, the burning-off of this would be an act of land-clearance, and might equally apply to burning stubble-fields in the autumn, for example.

[22] The OE has confused the Biblical order here. Fraud is repayable twofold and unlikely to be clearable on oath; but if a third party steals the money entrusted to a second party, then an oath might assert innocence. Perhaps some material was omitted here in the OE.

(here[23]) took it, or it perished (acwælc) of itself, and if he has proof (gewitnesse), he need not pay up (geldan). But if he has no proof, and *the original owner* does not believe (getriewe) him, let him make an oath (swerige) *to clear himself.*

29. If anyone seduce (beswice) an uncommitted woman (fæmnan unbeweddode) and sleeps with her, let him pay (forgielde) for her and take her then as his wife. But if the woman's father is unwilling to let her go (sellan), then let *the seducer* hand over money (agife fioh) in proportion to her dowry (æfter þæm weotuman).[24]

30. The women (fæmnan) who are accustomed to harbour enchanters (onfon gealdor-cræftigan) and wizards (scin-læcan) and witches (wiccan) – do not allow them to live.[25]

31. And he that has intercourse with animals (hæme mid netene) shall suffer death.

32. And he that sacrifices to idols (god-geldum onsæcge), rather than to God alone, let him suffer death.

33. Do not harass (geswenc) visitors from abroad (utan-cumene) and foreigners (elþeodige), for you were formerly strangers (elþeodige) on the land of the Egyptians.[26]

---

23 'Here' is likely to refer to Viking raiders in this context, and though the source of this provision is Exodus, there is no reason not to believe that the up-dated excuse was being used in Alfred's day.

24 Representing the Latin word 'dos', 'a marriage portion or dowry'.

25 The Vulgate has simply "Maleficos no patieris vivere" – Thou shalt not suffer evil-doers (implying magicians) to live (22:18). Presumably, Alfred is extending culpability to those who afford shelter to the evil-doers in order to undermine support for evil practices, and perhaps target the wealthier 'organisers' of crime. In specifying 'women', Alfred apparently had access to a reading like that which underlies the Authorised Bible's 'Thou shalt not suffer a witch to live.'

26 cf. Pref. ch.47. This clause was perhaps intended to encourage traders rather than raiders. Nonetheless, this and the following clause instil a sense of 'do unto others as you would have them do unto you', which is a substantial moral argument.

34. Do not harm (sceððan) widows and step-children (stiop-cild), neither do them any injury (deriað). If you do otherwise, they will call upon Me and I will listen to them, and then I will slay (slea) you with my sword and I will ensure that your wives shall be a widows and your children orphans (steop-cild).

35. If you hand over money (fioh selle) as a loan (to borge) to your comrade (geferan) who wishes to live with you, do not coerce him like an underling (niedling) and do not oppress (gehene) him with the interest (eacan).[27]

36. If someone has only a single garment to cover and clothe (werian) himself with and he hands it over (selle) as a pledge (to wedde), let it be returned before the sun sets. If you do not do so, then he will call unto Me, and I will listen to him because I am very clement (mild-heort).

37. Do not reproach your <u>Lord</u> (hlaford), nor curse the lord (hlaford) of the people (folces).[28]

38. Your tithe *i.e. tenth-part* <u>of profit</u> (sceattas) and your first-fruits of moving *animals* and growing *crops*, offer (agyf) to God.[29]

39. All the flesh that wild animals (wildeor) leave, do not eat it but give it to the dogs.

---

[27] This aims to distinguish between debt incurred as a penalty in law (which might involve slavery as a consequence) or genuine civil debt, and a friendly loan, which it is said should not be used to extract labour or impose unfree status.

[28] This version of the Vulgate Exodus 22:28 ("Diis non detrahes, et principi populi tui non maledices") takes 'diis' to mean 'God/Lord', not 'judges', as expected, in order to equate divine and secular power. However, the Revised Standard Version reinstates the reading 'God'. The New Testament is ambivalent: Matthew 22:21 divides God and Caesar, 1 Peter 2:17 says: 'Fear God. Honour the King.'

[29] The Bible also requires an offering or dedication to God of the first-born son, which is omitted here.

40. Do not bother to give credence (gehiranne) to the word of a false (leases) man, and do not approve his opinions (domas); do not repeat any of his assertions (gewitnesse).[30]

41. Do not join in (wend þu þe) the false judgement (unræd) and evil aspirations (unryht gewil) of the many (folces) *nor join* in their rumours (spræce) and outcry (geclysp), against your own conscience (ryht), <u>at the incitement of some ignorant person (þæs unwisestan lare). Do not support (geþafa) them.</u>[31]

42. If the stray cattle (giemeleas fioh) of another man come into your possession (on hand), though it be *the property of* your enemy, let him know about it.[32]

43. Judge (dem) equably (swiðe emne); do not lay down (dem) one rule (dom) for the rich, another for the poor; do not decide (dem) one *way* for a friend, another for a foe.[33]

44. Always shun falsehood (leasunga).

45. Never slay (acwele) a righteous (soð-fæstne) and innocent (unscildigne) man.

46. Never accept bribes (med-sceattum), for they very often blind the minds (geþoht) of wise men and pervert their words.

---

[30] Exodus 23:1 relates to not giving false evidence rather than to slanderous reports.

[31]'Folc' is here used in a derogatory sense, not the inclusive 'nation' of Pref. ch.37, but more representing an ignorant majority, almost an urban riot. 'Ryht' in this context suggests 'what you know to be sensible or proper', though here it rather encourages political quiescence. In the Vulgate the emphasis is different: it is in doing evil that you should not join the majority, nor give a false judgement simply because you are in a minority.

[32] This remained a very pertinent problem; cattle-raiding in border areas seems to have had almost the status of a sport and there is an OE charm designed to help recover missing cattle.

[33] This somewhat elaborates but preserves the spirit of the Biblical text.

47. Do not behave (læt) unkindly (uncuðlice) to foreigners (elþeodigan) and visitors from abroad (utan-cumenan); do not harass (drecce) them with unjust acts (mid unrihtum).[34]

48. Never swear an oath by (under) heathen gods, nor in any circumstances call upon them.[35]"

These are the regulations (domas) which the Almighty God himself spoke to Moses and ordered him to observe (to healdenne), and subsequently the only-born son of the Lord, our God, that is the Saviour Christ *confirmed, for* he said that he did not come to overturn these commandments (bebodu to brecanne)[36] nor to countermand *them*, but with every virtue (godum) to augment *them*, and he taught (lærde) clemency (mild-heortnesse) and humility (eadmodnesse). Then after his passion, before his apostles had dispersed throughout the world to teach,

---

[34] A slight elaboration of "peregrino molestus non eris"; cf. Pref. ch.33 above.

[35] This last provision comes from Exodus 23:13, and concludes the selection from the Book of the Covenant.

[36] After Matthew 5:17; "Think not that I come to destroy the Law, or the prophets: I am come not to destroy but to fulfil." and following verses. Later New Testament books, for example Paul's Letter to the Romans, are less convinced of the continuity between Old Testament and New Testament contexts, a point of view taken up by Ælfric in his Preface to Genesis. But here the more pertinent quotation would have been Matthew 22:37–40: "Jesus said unto him, 'Thou shalt love the Lord thy God with all thy heart, and with all thy soul, and with all thy mind. This is the first and great commandment. And the second is like unto it, Thou shalt love thy neighbour as thyself. On these two commandments hang all the Law and the Prophets." These inset quotations are both Old Testament in source, and the second is particularly poignant, for the very authority that Christ used to propose a concept of Law as positive good rather than a force negating evil was itself drawn from Levit. 19:18. "Thou shalt not avenge, nor bear any grudge against the children of thy people: but thou shalt love thy neighbour as thyself: I am the Lord." A place might also have been found for Matthew 7:1.

In terms of Alfred's law-code, however, what was needed was an argument tracing Law back to the earliest imaginable stage, hence his appeal to the Old Testament and consequent need to demonstrate the continuing validity of its teaching.

and while they were still together, many heathen nations turned to God. When they *i.e. the apostles* were all together, they sent messengers to Antioch and to Syria, to instruct them in Christ's law (æ). When *the apostles* realised that it was not having much effect (ne speow), they sent a written epistle to them. This is the letter that the apostles sent in unison to Antioch and to Syria and to Cilicia, which by now are turned from heathen nations to Christ:

"The apostles and the elder brethren wish you good health and we inform you that we have learned that some of our companions have reached you with our message and told you to keep a stricter *regime* than we instructed them to, and have much misled you with complex ordinances (gebodum), and have more confused than guided (gerihtan) your souls. Then we got together over this and it seemed best to us all that we should send Paul and Barnabas, men who would willingly give their lives (sawla) for God's name. With them we have sent Judas and Silas, to say the same to you. It seemed to the Holy Ghost and to us that we should not wish to place any burden on you beyond what was necessary for you to bear, that is that you forbear from worshipping idols (deofol-gyld), and do not partake of blood or strangled things, and forbear from fornication (dernum geligerum),[37] and that you wish other men should not do to you, you do not do to others."[38]

From this one precept (dom) one can learn that one should judge everyone fairly (on riht); one has no need of any other law-code

---

[37] The leniency of religious observation accepted here might be intended to appeal to the Vikings in England, for whom a sort of transitional Christianity would be of practical use?

[38] The last clause of this, though presented as part of the apostles' letter (Acts 15:23–29) is actually from the gospels: Luke 8:31 "And as ye would that men should do to you, do ye also to them likewise" and Matthew 7:12 "Therefore all things whatsoever ye would that men should do to you, do ye even so to them: for this is the Law and the Prophets." I can find no direct source for this in the Old Testament however, and it is a matter for reflection that in order to fit it into a law-code the New Testament text has to be put into a negative format.

(domboca).[39] Let him remember that he should not pronounce (deme) against any man *a sentence* that he would not wish someone else to pronounce against him, if that other sought judgement (dom) upon him *i.e. in similar circumstances.*

After that it happened that many nations accepted Christ's faith. Then there were many synods assembled throughout the world (middangeard) and likewise among the English (Angel-cyn) after they had accepted the faith of Christ, of the bishops and of other distinguished (geþungenra) wise men. Then they ordained (gesetton), of that clemency that Christ taught, that secular rulers (woruld-hlafordas) might, with their permission (leafan) *and* without reproach (synne), accept, for most misdeeds (misdæde), on the first offence (gylte), a monetary recompense (fioh-bote), which they then set. Except in *the case of* treason (hlaford-searwe), for which they dared not propose any clemency (mild-heortnesse), because Almighty God *i.e. Jesus* accorded (gedemde) none to them that handed him over to death; also he ordered *people* to love the lord as *they loved* themselves.[40] Then in many synods they ordained (gesetton) the penalty (bote) for many human misdeeds (misdæda), and in many synod-books wrote here one regulation (dom), there another.[41]

---

[39] The concept of a few-word summary replacing the Old Testament Law is found in Matthew 22:37–40 (quoted above), as in Romans 13:8 "Owe no man anything, but to love one another: for he that loveth another hath fulfilled the law." and Galatians 5:14 "For all the law is fulfilled in one word, even in this: 'Thou shalt love thy neighbour as thyself'."

[40] This seems a conflation of two texts: the commandment to love God (e.g. Deut. 6:5) and that of loving your neighbour as yourself. The word for lord in Latin (dominus) and OE (hlaford) is used equally of the deity as of a secular power, as in Modern English. This confusion has already been noted in Pref. ch.37 above. The authority for the death penalty for treason (incidentally still in force) cannot really be justified from the words or acts of Jesus, but may depend on a decree in a capitulary of a Papal legate in 786, either known directly or via Offa's Laws (see Dammery, 1990, vol.1, p.245).

[41] The line of argument here is that the Church canons provide a link between Biblical authority and secular Anglo-Saxon law. It is a train of thought seemingly derived from Fulk's Letter to Alfred (translated at Keynes and

Then I, King Alfred, collected these together and commanded many of them which our forefathers (foregengan) observed (heoldon) to be written out – those which appealed to me (me licode); and many of those that did not appeal to me I rejected, with the consent (geþeahte) of my Witan *or* commanded (bebead) them to be observed in a different way, for I did not dare to presume to set down (settan) anything much of my own in writing, because it was unknown to me how much of this would appeal to those who should come after us. But those *things* I encountered, either of the time of Ine, my kinsman, or of Offa, the king of the Mercians, or of Ethelbert, who first among the English (Angel-cynne) received baptism[42] – those which seemed to me most just (ryhtoste) I collected them together here, and omitted the rest.[43]

The Laws

[The Laws that follow are not usually considered among Alfred's major works, but must have been of considerable importance at the time and in succeeding reigns. The date of composition is unknown, but if the dependence on Fulk's letter is secure, and the date of that is 886–7, then the Laws could be the first of Alfred's 'authorial' ventures. An early date accords well with the need to assert royal authority through the

---

Lapidge pp.183–4). The diversity of such canons provides Alfred with a neat starting-point for his last paragraph to the Preface.

[42] For Alfred's borrowings see Liebermann (1916, vol.3 pp.35–36). Possible borrowings from Offa may affect Alfred's Laws ch.4, 8, 20, 37 and 41 (see Dammery, 1990, vol.1, p.239).

[43] A similar judicious attitude is found in the Leges Burgundionum prologue:

Cum de parentum nostrisque constitutionibus pro quiete et utilitate populi nostri inpensius cogitemus, quid potissimum de singulis causis et titulis honestati, disciplinae, rationi et iustitiae conveniret, et coram positis obtimatibus nostris universa pensavimus, et tam nostram quam eorum sententiam mansuris in eorum legibus sumpsimus statuta perscribi....

Wallace-Hadrill (1971, pp.34–35) points out further similarities with Rothari's and Liuvigild's 6th century Gothic Laws, all deriving this figure ultimately from Justinian's Seventh Novella.

establishment of a set of laws and is the sort of venture that might well be considered a priority.

Dammery (1990, vol.1, ch.3) argues against any authorial status for the rubrics (i.e. index of chapter headings, here omitted), in which he is backed by Thorpe (note to Alfred's Laws ch.22), but Dammery's further suggestion, that Ine's Laws might thus be connected with Alfred's Laws as a scribal decision rather than with any intent on Alfred's part (ibid. pp.15–16, 258–261 e.g. because they are contradictory in detail) is resolved already in Richards (1986) to whom "the codes of Alfred and Ine form a single, continuous, complete and up-to-date collection" (p.173), in which the more recent enactments take precedence. The issuing of Ine's Laws in conjunction with Alfred's would also help to stress the importance of tradition, West-Saxon rather than Kentish.

Indeed Alfred's aim (as per the Pastoral Care Preface) seems to have been to epitomise, almost restore, the past. With a Europe threatened by Vikings, its Holy Roman Empire about to break up, its Papacy in disarray, and his personal claim to the throne not without its critics, there was indeed little comfort in the present, and the past seems to have been evoked much as we today trust in progress and the future. To this end, precedent is especially important to Alfred (as we, conversely, today would promise benefits in the future from current policy!), and thus much of the material is customary provisions, with some central supervision to ensure their better working: that is, he seems to have set out to stabilise (or reassert?) a traditional society, and to this end was content to follow the format[44] and perhaps content of previous Laws.

Thus, Dammery identifies 'bold-getal' (Alfred Laws ch.37) and 'lefnes' (ch.8 and 20) as probably Mercian, and so perhaps deriving from Offa's (lost) Laws – 'þenden' (Laws ch.40) is unexpected, being a conventionally poetic conjunction but possibly also a Mercianism.

Many other words attest to the Alfredian period (not in dispute as the date of composition in this case), and among those typical of but not exclusive to Alfred are: 'gif þonne' (passim), 'læl' (Int.19), 'godgeldum' (Int.32), 'gehenan' (Int.35), 'afliemed' (Laws 1), 'esne' (Laws 43),

---

[44] Structurally, Alfred puts several important issues at the start and has his list of 'tariffs' near the end (ch.44–77), much as Ethelbert did. A detailed analysis is supplied by Dammery, 1990, vol.1, pp.247–253.

'asmored' (Int.49). Several may have direct links to Alfred's usage: 'aluc' (Int.13),[45] 'geclysp' 'outcry',[46] 'on nanum þingum' (Int.48),[47] 'woruld-hlafordas' (Int.49),[48] 'nehstan' (Int.13).[49] It may seem odd that such lexical points as are most typical of Alfred himself and his era are concentrated in the Introduction to the Laws, but a possible explanation is that the wording of the Laws themselves was to some extent formal and traditional, while the Introduction was a freer composition. While clearly Alfred would have read and approved the whole law-code, the lexical evidence would indicate that he quite possibly played a role in framing the introduction himself.]

Then I,[50] Alfred, king of the West-Saxons, showed these to all my councillors (witum), and they then said that it was agreeable (licode) to them all to observe *these laws*:

1. First we insist (lærað) that there is particular need that each person keep his oath (að) and his pledge (wed) carefully. If anyone be compelled to *give* either of these wrongly (on woh), either *to support* treachery to his lord (hlaford-searwe) or *to provide* any unlawful aid, then it is better to forswear than to fulfil. But if he pledge *himself* to that which it is right for him to fulfil and fails, let him submissively hand over his weapons and his possessions (æhta) to his friends to keep, and stay forty days in prison (carcerne)[51] in a property (tune) of the king. Let him undergo there

---

[45] See my note to Metre 12.28 in my edition of *Alfred's Metres of Boethius* (Pinner, 1991).

[46] Occurring in OE otherwise, as far as I can detect, only in Alfred's Pastoral Care (x2).

[47] See discussion in my *Alfred's Metres of Boethius* p.30.

[48] See discussion, ibid., p.29; the compound occurs also in Alfred's Pastoral Care.

[49] See discussion, ibid., note to Metre 4.12.

[50] Though the preface is in the first person, from hereon the plural 'we' is standard, implying either the king as representative of the nation or the king acting in unison with his Witan.

[51] This is the first surviving reference to prison in OE texts, I believe. It is not, however, as place of confinement in the modern sense, but rather a neutral area, guaranteed by the king, where the accused can await some resolution of

whatever the bishop prescribes *as penance* (scrife), and let his kinsmen (mægas) feed him if he himself has no food. If he has no kin, or has no food, let the king's officer (gerefa) feed him. If one has to compel him to this *i.e. to surrender*, and otherwise he is unwilling *to co-operate* – if they have to bind him, he shall forfeit (þolige) his weapons and his possessions (ierfes). If he is slain *?while resisting*, let him lie uncompensated (or-gilde). If he makes an escape before the time *is up*, and he is *re*captured, let him stay forty days in prison as he would have previously. But if he gets away, let him be banished (afliemed) and excommunicated from all the churches of Christ. Further, if someone has provided surety (borh) for him, let him compensate (bete) for the breach of surety (borg-bryce) as custom (ryht) require him, and *atone* for the breach of pledge (wed) as his confessor imposes in his case.

2. If anyone seek out *as sanctuary* for any offence (scylde) any of the monastic houses (mynster-hama) to which the king's revenue (feorm) applies, or any other exempt community (hiered) that is worthy of respect (ar-wyrðe), he shall have a period of three days of immunity (to gebeorganne), unless he wants to negotiate (þingian) *before that*. If someone harms (geyflige) him during that period, either by assault (slege) or by fettering him (mid bende), or by a penetrating wound (þurh-wunde), let *the aggressor* pay compensation (bete) for each of such *attacks* according to proper practice (mid ryhte þeodscipe), both with wergeld (were) and with a fine (wite), and 120 shillings to that community (hiwum), as compensation (bote) *for breach of* sanctuary (ciric-friðes), and let his own *possessions* (agne) be forfeit (forfongen).[52]

3. If anyone violate (abrece) the king's surety (borg), let him pay compensation for the *original* charge (tyht) as customary law (ryht)

---

the case. The problem, already noticed here, is of course who pays for this 'service'?

[52] The MSS have two readings, suggesting either that his possessions should or should not be forfeit. The latter is clearly more in keeping with the seriousness of the offence of breach of sanctuary, which is given such prominence in the law-code.

direct, and for the violation of surety (borge-bryce) with five pounds of the purer pennies (mærra pæninga). *In the case of* breach of an archbishop's surety (borges-bryce) or protection (mundbyrd), let him compensate (gebete) with three pounds. For violation of the surety or protection of another bishop or official (ealdormonnes), let him make compensation (gebete) with two pounds.[53]

4. If anyone plot (sierwie) against the king's life (feorh), either directly (þurh hine) or by harbouring outlaws (wreccena) or *indirectly* through the agency of his men (manna), let him be liable with his life (feores scyldig) and with all that he owns (age). If he desire *to prove himself* loyal (triowan), let him do *that* by *paying* a king's wergeld (wergelde). Similar *protection* we ordain (settað) for all ranks (hadum), both common (ceorle) and noble (eorle): whoever plots against his master's life shall be liable with his life and with all that he owns – or let him show his loyalty (getriowe) by *paying* his master's wergeld (were).

5. Also we appoint (settað) to every church that a bishop has consecrated this *right of* sanctuary (frið): that if a party to a feud (fah-mon) run or ride *to the church, then* no one may drag him forth (ut teo) for seven days. If however anyone does that, then let him be liable (scyldig) *at the rate of breach of* a king's protection (mundbyrde) and *at the rate of breach of* church sanctuary (cirican

---

[53] Having provided for a 'cooling off' period, in which some negotiation of a case can take place, and insisted that anyone so lodged in the king's or the church's keeping must be safe from attack, in this clause it is also insisted that there must be good conduct from such a 'refugee', and that anyone re-offending during such a period be heavily penalised (corresponding to modern breach of bail, though no freedom of movement is implied in using 'bail' in the translation). The person providing the 'accommodation' for the 'prisoner' becomes in effect the guarantor or supervisor of that offender's good conduct, so that re-offence involves not only further action in law but a fine on that offender payable to the 'guarantor'. The bond implicit between protected and protector is called both 'borg' (a financial guarantee) and 'mundbyrd' (personal supervision), though what is involved is presumably a concept rather than an actual financial or personal arrangement.

friðes) – more if he take more from the site.[54] [*And the sanctuary-seeker shall be safe*] if he can survive hunger, *and* unless he himself *try to* fight his way out. If the community have greater (maran) need of their church, let them keep (healde) him in another building (ærne), and let that not have the more doors than the church *itself*.[55] Let the church official (cirican ealdor) ensure (gewite) that no one gives *the sanctuary-seeker* food during that period. If he himself is willing to hand over (ut-rǣcan) his weapons to his foes (gefan), let *them* keep him for 30 days and inform his kin (mǣgum) about him.[56] Also *it shall count as* sanctuary (cirican frið) if some man seek out a church about any offence (gylta) that had not previously been revealed, and there confess himself in God's name – let *the penalty* be half remitted. He that steal (stalað) on Sunday (Sunnan niht) or at Yule or at Easter or on Holy Thursday or on the Rogation days (Gang-dagas) – for each of those we intend that there should be a double-penalty (twy-bote), as during Lent.

6. If anyone steal (geþeofige) something in a church, let him pay (forgylde) a plain compensation (angylde) and the fine (wite) such as *they* consider appropriate to the plain compensation, and let them strike (slea) the hand off with which he did it *i.e. the deed*. If he wishes to redeem (alysan) his hand, and they consent to that, let him pay (gelde) in proportion to his wergeld (were).

7. If anyone fights in the king's hall (healle) or draw his weapon, and he is seized, let *the penalty* be at the king's judgement (dome), either death or life (lif), as he is willing to grant (forgifan) him. If he

---

[54] The text here may well, as Thorpe notes, be corrupt; at the end of this sentence there seems the implication that the penalty for breach of sanctuary could be even greater if damage or theft accompanies an attempt to get at a 'prisoner'. In the next sentence, I have supplied an opening clause, as here we seem to be resuming the topic of safety mentioned earlier.

[55] Presumably for security on both sides: that the 'prisoner' might not be got at the easier, nor evade his pursuers the easier. Might church towers be suitable?

[56] So that food could then be brought?

escapes (losige) and is captured later, let him pay (forgielde) in proportion to his wergeld (wergilde), and atone (gebete) for the offence (gylt) with wergeld and fine (swa wer swa wite), as he may deserve by his act (gewyrht age).

8. If anyone abducts (ut-alæde) a nun of a nunnery (mynstre) without the king's or bishop's leave (lefnesse), let him pay (geselle) 120 shillings, half to the king, half to the bishop and the church patron (cirican hlaforde) who had charge of (age) the nun. If she lives longer than he that abducted her, let her not have any of his estate (ierfes). If she bears a child, let that not have any more of the estate than the mother. If anyone slay (ofslea) her child, let him pay (gielde) the king[57] the maternal kindred's (medren-mæga) share; to the paternal kin (fæder-mægum) let him pay (agife) their share.

9. If anyone slay (ofslea) a woman (wif) with child, while the child still be within her, let him pay full compensation (gielde) for the woman (wif-man), and half compensation (gelde) for the child according to the wergeld (were) of the father's kin (fæder-cnosles).

Let the fine *payable to the king* always be 60 shillings, until the *corresponding* simple compensation (angylde) rises to 30 shillings. When the simple compensation rises to that *level*, then let the fine (wite) be 120 shillings. Formerly there was *a defined fine* for a gold-thief (gold-þeof), and a horse-thief (stod-þeofe) and a bee-thief (beo-þeofe) and many *special* fines (witu) greater than others. Now all are alike except for an illegal slaver (man-þeofe) *and that is* 120 shillings.[58]

---

[57] i.e. not to the mother or her kin. This as retribution, I assume, for the breach of the vow of chastity, though whether the nun went willingly or reluctantly would have seemed relevant here. Perhaps however the apparent harshness is also intended to discourage nuns from contemplating marriage.

[58] This second clause clearly distinguishes between the compensation due to the victim or victim's kin, by virtue of their loss, and the fine payable to the king, by virtue of breach of his peace or laws. The two are connected on a sort of sliding scale (as indicated for example in ch.6 above), which is explained here.

10. If a man has intercourse (hæme) with the wife of a 1200 *shilling wergeld* man, let him pay in compensation (gebete) 120 shillings to the husband (were). For a 600 *shilling wergeld* man *i.e. husband*, let him pay in compensation 100 shillings. For a common (cierliscum) man *i.e. husband*, let him make compensation of 40 shillings.

11. If someone grabs the breast (breost) of a common woman (cirliscere fæmnan), let him compensate (gebete) with five shillings. If he throws her *to the ground* (oferweorpe) but (ond) does not have sexual intercourse (gehæme) with her, let him compensate (gebete) with 60 shillings. If he has sexual intercourse with *her*, let him compensate (gebete) with sixty shillings. If some other man had previously lain (læge) with her, then let the compensation (bot) be half that. If someone accuse (teo) her *of complicity*, let her clear (geladie) *herself with an oath guaranteed* by sixty hides (hida) *of land,* or forfeit (þolige be) half the compensation (bote).[59] If this happens to a nobly born woman (æđel-borenan wifman), let the compensation (bot) increase (weaxe) in proportion to the wergeld (were).

12. If someone burns (bærneđ) or cuts down (heaweđ) another person's trees (wudu) without permission (unaliefedne), let him pay over (forgielde) 5 shillings for each substantial tree (great treow), and thereafter, no matter how many there are, five pence (pæningum) for each *tree*, and thirty shillings as a fine (wite).

13. In the course of their joint work (gemænan weorce) *felling trees*, if someone is killed (offelle) by accident (ungewealdes), let the tree (treow) *involved* be given to his kin (mægum), and let them remove

---

[59] The problem here is one still encountered in law: the presumption that a woman who is raped in some sense partly responsible. Nonetheless, in OE Law, if the act is forcible, whatever else mitigates, a substantial penalty results.

(hæbben) it off the property (lande) within 30 days; otherwise let him possess (fo) it that owns (age) the forest (wudu).[60]

14. If someone is born dumb or deaf, so that he can neither deny (onsecggan) nor confess (andettan) his sins (synna), let the father make compensation (bete) for his misdeeds (misdæda).[61]

15. If someone fights or draws his weapon in the presence of (beforan) an archbishop, let him make compensation (gebete) with 150 shillings. If this occurs (belimpe) before another bishop or royal official (ealdormen) let him make compensation (gebete) with 100 shillings.

16. If someone steals (forstele) a cow or mare (stod-myran) and drives off (of adrife) a foal or calf, let him pay over (forgelde) one shilling *as well as paying compensation for* the adult animals (moder) according to their value (weorðe).[62]

17. If anyone entrust a child (un-magan)[63] into *the keeping of* others, and he *i.e. the offspring* die (forferie) while in that guardianship

---

[60] This clause might be called a provision for 'industrial compensation', and presumably applied to cases other than that of tree felling, which is used here as a classic example. A loss of person and income has occurred, which it seems right to compensate in some way, but not within criminal proceedings: the occurrence was accidental, but nonetheless would not have taken place had the man not been working in dangerous circumstances. Concepts of negligence on either side affecting liability are not invoked.

[61] The concept here is that the father should be liable for any penalties incurred by a child that is born at a disadvantage, presumably because a defect at birth was attributed to some paternal sin. Interestingly, the responsibility does not involve the mother or the kindred.

[62] A young animal is dependent on its mother, so to steal the adult animal while leaving the offspring behind involves a double loss, which is recognised here i.e. an act involves responsibility for contingent effects. Compare ch.9 above.

[63] Here I translate 'unmaga' as child, following Thorpe, in the sense of non-adult rather than a disadvantaged child; it could indeed reflect a possible practice of adoption of any child by a wealthier member of the kindred. (Such fostering was common in Irish society, where it was equivalent to education – see Dillon and Chadwick *The Celtic Realms*, London, 1973,

(fæstinge), let him that did the fostering (fede hine) prove his innocence (getriowe hine) of any crime (facnes), if anyone accuse (teo) him of it.

18. If anyone grabs at (gefo) a nun's clothing (hrægl) or breast (breost) with sexual intent (hæmed-þinge), unless with her consent (leafe), let him pay double *the rate of* compensation (twy-bete) we previously arranged (funden) for a lay-person (læwdum men).[64] If she[65] commit adultery (forlicgge) and she is a betrothed woman (weddodu fæmne), if she is a commoner (cirlisc), let 60 shillings be paid in compensation (gebete) to the guarantor (byrgean), and let that be in livestock (cwic-æhtum) *or* cattle (feo-godum), but let no one give (selle) any human (mon) as part of it.[66] If she be of 600 *shilling wergeld*, let 100 shillings be paid in compensation (geselle) to the guarantor (byrgean). If she be of 1200 *shilling wergeld*, let compensation of 120 shilling be paid (gebete) to the guarantor (byrgean).

19. If anyone lends (onlæne) his weapon to another so that he may kill (ofslea) with it, they may combine, if they are willing, *in the matter of paying* the wergeld (were). If they are unwilling to co-operate, let him that proffered (onlah) the weapon pay (gielde) a third part of the wergeld (weres) and a third part of the fine (wites). If he *i.e.*

---

p.133.) Whatever the context here, the point is that the guardian bears legal responsibility for the child, and must answer for that, whatever the child's background.

[64] This is in part an ecclesiastical version of ch.11.

[65] This represents the plural pronoun 'hie' in the OE, though the following verb 'forlicgge' is singular. To add to the uncertainty the OE text does not specify the subject of the verb 'gebete', so it is not clear whether it is the woman who must pay compensation, the couple together, or the seducer alone. Nor is it clear (to us) who the guarantor (byrgea) is, the man who paid over any betrothal money (i.e. the cheated husband) or the holder of that money (i.e. the woman's kin).

[66] The exclusion of a human (Thorpe and Whitelock take it to mean 'a slave') from being part of any compensation payment may refer to the temptation to offer the child of such a misalliance as compensation for the misdeed.

the loaner of the weapon prefer to clear (triewian) himself *and assert* that he knew of no evil-intent (facn) in *making* the loan (læne), he may do so.[67]

If a sword-polisher (sweord-hwita) accept (onfo) another man's weapon for refurbishment (to feormunge), or a smith *take on* a tool (andweorc) of someone's *to repair*, let both return (agifan) it in good condition (gesund),[68] equivalent to that in which either of them earlier received (onfeng) it – unless either of them had before stipulated (þingode) that he need not be responsible for its full value (angylde healdan ne þorfte).[69]

20. If someone entrust (oðfæste) cattle (feoh) to another man's monk, without the approval (lefnesse) of the patron of that monk, and it gets lost (losige), let he that originally owned (ahte) it suffer *the loss*.[70]

21. If a priest (preost) slay (ofslea) another man, let all that he *i.e. the priest* brought into the monastic community (ham) be turned over (weorpe) to the possession (to handa) *of the victim's representatives,* and let the bishop unfrock (unhadige) him; then he shall be removed (agife hine) from the monastery, unless the civil patron (hlaford) intercede for him.

---

[67] The owner of the weapon is involved not only because of his contributory guilt, in letting someone else have the use of a dangerous item, but presumably because weapons would often bear some inscription making them easily traceable. Possibly also a weapon was deemed to have some special relation to the owner that involved him in some symbolic way to acts done with it (cf. sword in *Beowulf* 1137+). In this clause, an attempt is made to define the level of contributory guilt.

[68] Whitelock translates this 'unstained' i.e. 'without it having been used to commit a crime'; this is possible if the link with the preceding clause is strong – but there could equally be a link with the simple sort of transfer covered in the following clause.

[69] Presumably when an article is so damaged that its repair could not be guaranteed.

[70] A monk, in effect, cannot be responsible in 'civil law', unless a civil patron of the monastery is involved in a transaction.

22. If someone wishes in the local assembly (folces gemot) to declare (geyppe) a claim for debt (eofot)[71] to the king's officer (gerefan), and then wishes to cancel (geswican) it, let him impute (gestæle) *i.e. transfer* it to a truer source (on ryhtran hand) if he can. If he cannot, let him forfeit (þolie) the single value (angyldes).

23. If a dog rends (toslite) or bites (abite) someone, for the first misdeed (misdæde) let *the owner* hand over (geselle) 6 shillings, if he is *still* giving it food.[72] For a second occurrence (cerre), *let him give* 12 shillings, and for a third, 30 shillings. If, upon any of these misdeeds, the dog escapes (losige), nonetheless the penalty (bot) proceeds. If the dog commit (gewyrce) more misdeeds and he *i.e. the owner* still keeps (hæbbe) him, let him pay compensation (bete) at the level of a full wergeld (be fullan were) as well as wound-compensation according to what he *i.e. the dog* has done (swa he wyrce).

24. If an ox (neat) wounds someone, let him *i.e. the owner* hand the animal (neat) over or come forward with some solution (fore-þingie).

25. If someone forces (geþreated) a commoner's slave-woman (ceorles mennen) to sexual intercourse (to ned-hæmde), let him compensate (gebete) the owner (ceorl) with 5 shillings and *pay* 60 shillings fine (to wite). If a male slave (þeow-mon) compel (genede) a female slave (þeowne) to sexual intercourse (ned-hæmde), let him atone (bete) with his testicles (eowende).[73]

26. If someone force (geþreatige) an underage woman (ungewintrædne wifmon) into sexual intercourse (nied-hæmde), let the

---

[71] Whitelock in *EHD* extends the meaning to any charge.

[72] The implication seems to be, if it is still truly a domestic dog, and not one that has run wild and is no longer connected with a human master. This clause looks at the general responsibility for domestic animals as Pref. ch.21 dealt with the case of dangerous livestock.

[73] There is no mention, it is notable, of any compensation to the raped female slave – her rights would be deemed to be vested in the master.

compensation (bot) be as that of an adult person (gewintredan monnes).

27. If someone without kin on his father's side (fæder-mæga mægleas) gets into a fight (gefeohte) and kills (ofslea) someone, if he has maternal relatives (medren-mægas), let them pay (gieldan) a third part of the wergeld (weres); *and* a third part his guild-brethren (gegyldan); for a third part *unpaid* let him flee (fleo). If he has no maternal relatives, let the guild-brethren pay a half; for a half *unpaid* let him flee.[74]

28. If someone kill (ofslea) a man so circumstanced (geradne mon) *and* if he has no kinfolk, let them pay (gield) half *the wergeld* to the king, half to his guild-brethren (gegildan).

29. If anyone in a group (hloðe) kills a 200 *shilling wergeld* man *who is* guiltless (unsynnigne), let him that acknowledges the blow (slæges andetta) pay over (gielde) wergeld (wer) and fine (wite), and let every man who was of the party (on siðe) hand over (geselle) 30 shillings in token of his complicity (to hloð-bote).

30. If it is *a case of* a 600 *shilling wergeld* man, *let* each of them *pay* 60 shillings as a token of their complicity (to hloð-bote), and let him that struck the *fatal* blow (se slaga) *pay* wergeld (wer) and fine (wite).

31. If he *that is killed* is a 1200 *shilling wergeld man*, let each of them *pay* 120 shillings, and *let* the one who struck the *fatal* blow (se slaga) *pay* wergeld (wer) and fine (wite). If a group (hloð) commit this *sort of killing*, and later deny *responsibility* on oath (oðswerian), let them all be accused (tio man hie ealle), and let them pay over (forgieldan) the wergeld (wer) as a group

---

[74] The idea is, kinfolk, paternal or maternal, or the work-group, shall be liable for the wergeld in part, even if the aggressor himself cannot manage his contribution but is declared an outlaw.

(gemænum hondum), and together pay one fine (wite) such as corresponds to the wergeld (wer).[75]

32. If someone commits slander (folc-leasunge gewyrce) and it is proved against him (on hine geræf), let him make atonement (gebete) with no lighter penalty (leohtran þinge) than having his tongue cut out. It *i.e. the tongue* must not be redeemed (lesan) for any lesser value (undeorran weorðe) than would be reckoned (mon ge-eahtige) in proportion to the wergeld (were).

33. If someone reproach (oncunne) another with *breach of* church-witnessed pledge (god-borges) and wishes to accuse (tion) him of not fulfilling (gelæste) any (hwelcne) of those *pledges* that he gave (gesealde) him, let *the accuser* make his preliminary oath (fore-að) in four churches, and the other *i.e. the accused*, if he wishes to assert his good faith (hine treowian) – let him do that in twelve churches.

34. Also it is laid down (gereht) for traders (ciepe-monnum) that they should produce (gebrengan) before the king's officer (kyninges gerefan) at the local assembly (on folc-gemote) those people (men) that they are taking (læden) inland with them, and let it be established (gerecce) how many of them there are. And let them take (nimen) *only* such men as they can afterwards be accountable for (to ryhte brengan) at the local assembly. And if they have need of more men along with them on their journey (fore), let it always be declared (gecyðe), as often as is necessary, to the king's officer before the assembly (in gemotes gewitnesse).[76]

---

[75] The point here is to ensure that compensation is not avoided because an individual member of a group refuses to own up to the fatal blow. In that case the compensation is payable communally.

[76] The object of this seems to be two-fold: that merchants should not be allowed to move around with more men than is strictly necessary (or they might constitute a raiding party?), and that there should be some 'quality control' on who is employed in such work, with the merchant taking responsibility for them; but secondly that the number should be counted, presumably to guard against unauthorised slaving.

35. If someone restrains a free man (cierliscne mon gebinde) *who is* innocent (unsynnigne), let him pay compensation (gebete mid) of ten shillings. If he flogs (beswinge) him, *compensation of* twenty shillings. If he put him to torture (on hengenne, variant: asnæse),[77] *compensation of* thirty shillings. If as a humiliation (on bismor) he shaves *his head* like a ------- (homolan),[78] let him pay compensation of ten shillings. If he shaves him *i.e. his head* like a priest's, without binding him (unbundenne) let him pay compensation of thirty shillings. If he shaves off his beard, let him pay compensation of twenty shillings. If he ties him up (gebinde) and then shaves *his head* like a priest's, let him pay compensation of sixty shillings.[79]

36. It is also established (gefunden) that if someone has a spear (spere) over *his* shoulder and someone else impales (on-asnased) himself *upon it*, he *i.e. the spear-carrier* shall pay (gielde) the wergeld (wer) without any fine (wite). If he is impaled from in front (beforan eagum), let him *i.e. the spear-carrier* pay (gielde) the wergeld (wer). If someone accuses (tio) him *i.e. the spear-carrier* of deliberately doing it (gewealdes on þære dæde), let him assert his innocence (getriowe) at a rate corresponding to the fine (be wite), and by that finish with (afelle) the fine (wite). And this applies if the point (ord) is above[80] the rest of the shaft (hindeweard sceaft);

---

[77] BT, under the heading 'hengen III' discuss possible meanings: the sense 'prison' is attested, and 'stocks' has been suggested here; but its root in 'hanging', extended often to mean 'crucifixion' suggests something more brutal; the variant 'asnæse' is used of the action of impaling.

[78] The meaning of 'homolan' is uncertain: the verb 'hamelian' means 'to mutilate', so the noun must reflect something unpleasant – the state of castration?

[79] The humiliation seems to rest on a shaved head as a ritual of abnormality, "an ignominious punishment inflicted upon slaves, and offenders of the worst class ...also the mark of a madman or fool." (Thorpe). The heads of all prisoners in British prisons were close cropped until 1930, a fashion used subsequently to indicate an unpopular prisoner.

[80] Or if the point is three fingers breadth higher than the shaft, in a variant.

if they are both level (gelic), point and shaft, let it count as no risk (sie butan pleo).[81]

37. If someone wants to seek a *new* lord (hlaford), *transferring* from one district (bold-getæl) to another district, let him do it with the knowledge of the chief officer (ealdormonnes gewitnesse) to whom he was originally responsible (þe he ær folgode) in his shire. If he does it without his *i.e. the officer's* knowledge, let him who harbours (feormie) him as his follower (to men) pay over (geselle) 120 shillings as a fine (to wite). But let him divide (dæle) *it, paying* the king half in the shire (scire) where the man was originally answerable (ær folgode), and half in that he has moved to. If he *i.e. the man who moves* had done anything wrong (hwæt yfla) where he came from (ær wæs), let him who receives (onfo) him as his follower (to men) pay the compensation (gebete) and a fine (wite) of 120 shillings to the king.[82]

---

[81] This is a prime example of a seemingly pointless enactment, for accidents of this kind cannot have been that common (though entirely possible), and scarcely seem to deserve a chapter to the exclusion of many other possible dangerous circumstances. It has been suggested that it reflects a particular judgement in a particular case, and was recorded for its intrinsic interest. But surely it is included because it represents a theory of responsibility that can be applied to all sorts of similar cases i.e. if the holder of any dangerous article takes some care to keep it out of the way, he cannot be held responsible, but if he is negligent or careless, then he contributes to any consequent accident. Because of the special circumstances, the fine is remitted; also perhaps the king would not care to benefit from a mishap that might be likeliest to occur among his own troops.

[82] This raises some questions about exactly how 'free' a freeman was. But its main point seems to have been to encourage the population to settle after the inevitable fluidity of the period of Viking raids (though there is a similar provision in Ine ch.39 "If anyone travels without permission away from his lord..."). Also it covers the problem of an offender fleeing to another area: thus the division of the compensation. To apply to evaders in the Danelaw a treaty rather than a West Saxon law would be needed (and was separately undertaken), but the provision here might apply to a semi-independent region like Mercia.

38. If someone starts a fight (gefeohte) in front of the king's officer (ealdormen) at an assembly (on gemote), let him pay compensation (bete) of wergeld (wer) and a fine (wite), as it is customary (ryht sie); and as a priority (beforan þam) a fine of 120 shillings to the officer (ealdormen) *concerned.* If he disturb (arære) the assembly (folc-gemot) by drawing a weapon, *let him pay* 120 shillings to the officer by way of fine (to wite). If something of this sort occurs (gelimpe) before the king's officer's deputy (gingran) or a royal priest (cyninges preoste), *let him pay* 30 shillings by way of fine (to wite).

39. If someone starts a fight (gefeohte) on the floor of a free man's house (on cierlisces monnes flette), let him pay compensation of six shillings to the freeman (ceorle). If he draws his weapon but does not fight (no feohte), let *the compensation* be half that. If either *of these offences* takes place *in the house of a* 600 *shilling wergeld man,* let *the rate* rise to triple the compensation (bote) due the freeman. *In the case of a* 1200 shilling wergeld man, *a rate* twice that of the compensation (bote) of the 600 *shilling wergeld man.*

40. For breaking into a royal residence (burg-bryce) *the penalty* shall be 120 shillings. *Into* an archbishop's, ninety shillings. *Into* another bishop's or a royal officer's (ealdormonnes), 60 shillings. *Into* a 1200 *shilling wergeld* man's, thirty shillings. *Into* a 600 *shilling wergeld* man's, fifteen shillings. For breaking into a freeman's property (edor-bryce) *the penalty* shall be five shillings. If something of this kind takes place (gelimpe) while (þenden) the levy (fyrd) is on duty elsewhere (ute sie),[83] or during Lent, let it be a double compensation (twy-bote). If someone sets aside (alecgge) holy custom (halig ryht) publicly (in folce) in Lent without an

---

[83] The 'fyrd' represented a levy of all weapon-bearing freemen (in theory), so to commit a robbery while the men of a community were elsewhere on necessary duty had to be dealt with specially.

exemption (butan leafe), let him pay a compensation (gebete mid) of 120 shillings.[84]

41. The man who has charter land (boc-land)[85] *which* his kin (mægas) left (leafden) him, is not allowed (ne moste), we enact (we setton), to part with it (sellan) outside his kin-group (mæg-burge), if there is written evidence (gewrit) or spoken witness (gewitnes) that it was forbidden (forbod wære) to be done by those people (manna) who originally acquired (gestrindon) it or by those who passed (sealdon) it to him. Let him *i.e. the one who opposes the alienation process* declare (gerecce) *any such stipulation* in the presence (on gewitnesse) of the king and the bishop, with his own kin attending.

42. Also we command (we beodað) that the man who knows his enemy (gefan) is quiescent at home (ham-sittende) should not start a fight (ne feohte) before he has asked him for justice (ryhtes). If he has the strength (mægnes) to surround (beride) his enemy and besiege (inne besitte) him, let him contain (gehealde) him for 7 days within and not attack him (hine on ne feohte) if he *i.e. the enemy* is willing to abide (geþolian) within. After seven days if he is willing to surrender (on hand gan) and hand over his weapons, let him *i.e. the avenger* keep him unharmed (gehealde hine gesundne) for thirty days and inform (gebodie) his kinsmen (mægum) and his friends about him. But if he *i.e. the enemy* flee (ge-irne) to a church, let *the matter be resolved* according to the privilege of the church, as we detailed above.[86] But if he *i.e. the avenger* does not have the resources (mægenes) to besiege him *i.e. the enemy*, let him ride to the royal officer (ealdormen) and ask him for help (fultumes). If he

---

[84] This last clause is an unusual secular enforcement of a religious practice (Lent having special rules e.g. fasting); but it is not clear to whom the penalty would be paid – king or Church?

[85] 'Bookland' was so called because its ownership and status was recorded in writing. Its ownership was thus theoretically private and personal, but in practice, all of a kin-group had some stake in such property, and their interests are protected in this clause, 'bookland' being an innovation and thus arguably outside standard kin custom.

[86] See Laws ch.7.

i.e. the officer is unwilling to assist (fultumian), let him ride *and ask* the king, before he mounts an attack (feohte).

Further, if someone happen upon his enemy (gefan) and did not know beforehand that he was quiescent at home, if he *i.e. the enemy* is willing to hand over (sellan) his weapon*s*, let him be held for thirty days and inform his friends about him; if he is not willing to hand over his weapons then he *i.e. the avenger* may attack (foethan on) him. If he *i.e. the enemy* is willing to surrender (on hand gan) and hand over his weapons and yet someone still attacks him (on him feohte), let *the aggressor* pay over wergeld (wer) and wound *compensation*, according to what he has done (swa he gewyrve), and *pay* a fine (wite), and lose his kin-status (hæbbe his mæg forworht).

We also declare (cweðað) someone may fight in support of his lord (mid his hlaforde) without blame (orwige), if anyone has attacked (on fiohte) the lord; so too the lord may fight in support of his follower (mid þy men). In the same way, someone may fight on behalf of his blood relative (geborene mæge) if someone attack (onfeohtað) him wrongfully (on woh), but not *take the side of a kinsman* against his lord – that we do not permit (ne liefað). Someone may fight blamelessly (orwige) if he discovers another with his lawful wife (æt his æwum wife) behind closed doors (betynedum durum) or under the one cover (reon), or with his legitimate (æwum-borenre) daughter, or with his legitimate sister or with his mother *if* she was given (forgifen) lawfully (to æwum) to his father.[87]

---

[87] The length of this chapter indicates the complexity and perhaps the importance of this issue i.e. the tendency to strike out and gain revenge without giving the processes (customary or legal) of settlement a chance. The right of a co-operative 'defendant' to have the more conciliatory option observed is upheld here, and to be enforced if possible by the king's officers, a new element perhaps in feud settlement, aimed perhaps not so much to weaken the role of the kin system in justice (for no other process of prosecution was available) but to reserve for central authority the right to intervene. But in some cases it is recognised that instant action is justifiable. The natural right of self-defence is extended to let someone help a kinsman

43. To all free people (frioum monnum) let these *following* days be granted (forgiefene) *as holidays* but not to slaves (þeowumn mannum) and servile workers (esne-wyrhtum): twelve days at Christmas (Ʒehol), and the day that Christ overcame (oferswiðde) the Devil,[88] and St Gregory's commemoration day (gemynd-dæg),[89] and seven days before Easter and seven after, and one day at the celebration (tide) of St. Peter and St. Paul,[90] and the full week in harvest before St. Mary's Mass,[91] and one day for the celebration of All Hallows.[92] The four Wednesdays in the Ember weeks shall be granted (forgifen) to all slaves to sell (sellanne) to anyone that it pleases them to anything either that any man will give them in God's name or what they in any spare time (hwil-sticcum) can manage (ge-earnian).

44. As compensation (to bote) for a head-wound (heafod-wunde): if both bones (of the head) be pierced (þyrel), let *the aggressor* pay (geselle) him thirty shillings. If the outer bone *only* be pierced, fifteen shillings compensation.

45. If in *the area of* the hair (feaxe) there is a wound (wund) an inch long, let *the aggressor* give (geselle) one shilling in compensation (to bote). If in front of the hair there is a wound an inch long, two shillings as compensation.

46. If someone strikes off (ofaslea) the other[93] ear, let him give 30 shillings in compensation. If the hearing be affected (oðstande) so

---

or a master, and to avenge a blood relation, but not to avenge 'in hot blood' lesser degrees of relationship, and here illegitimacy/concubine status etc. is taken to weaken such a relationship.

[88] 15 February.

[89] 12 March

[90] 29 June

[91] 15 August

[92] 1 November

[93] Thorpe plausibly suggests a clause, comparable to Ethelbert 39, is lacking here for the first ear. However, compare the opening formula of the following clause.

that he cannot hear (gehieran), let him *i.e. the aggressor* give (geselle) 60 shillings in compensation.

47. If someone put out (ofaslea) another man's eye, let him pay in compensation (to bote) 60 shillings and 6 shillings and 6 pennies and a third of a penny.[94] If it *i.e. the eye* stay in the head but he can see nothing with it, let a third part of the compensation (bote) be remitted (stande inne).

48. If someone strikes off (ofaslea) another man' nose (neb), let him compensate him with 60 shillings.

49. If someone strike out (ofaslea) another man's tooth at the front of his head, let him compensate it with 8 shillings; if it is a back tooth (wong-tođ), let him give 4 shillings in compensation. A man's canine tooth (tux) is worth 15 shillings.

50. If someone rends (forslihđ) a man's cheeks so that they *i.e. the muscles?* are severed (forode), let him compensate with 15 shillings. A man's chin-bone, if it be broken (toclofen), let *the aggressor* give 12 shillings in compensation.

51. If someone's windpipe (þrot-bolla) is perforated (þyrel), let *the aggressor* pay compensation of 12 shillings.

52. If someone's tongue is removed (don) from his head by another's actions (dædum), let that be the same as compensation for an eye.

53. If someone is wounded in the shoulder so that the muscle fluid (liđ-seaw)[95] flow out (ut-flowe), let *the aggressor* make compensation with 30 shillings.

54. If the arm is shattered (forad) above the elbow, in that case 15 shillings must *be paid* in compensation.

55. If the arm-bones (earm-scancan)[96] be both shattered (forade), the compensation (bot) shall be 30 shillings.

---

[94] Not an obviously lucky figure.

[95] BT suggest 'synovia' as the medical term; an injury affecting the interior of the muscle is clearly indicated, at any rate.

[96] Either above and below the elbow, or perhaps the two bones of the forearm.

56. If the thumb is struck off (ofaslægen), for that (þam) must 30 shillings *be paid* in compensation.

    If the nail is struck off, for that (þam) they must *pay* 5 shillings in compensation.

57. If the fore finger (scyte-finger) is struck off, let the compensation be 15 shillings; for the nail let it be 4 shillings.

58. If the middle finger be struck off, the compensation shall be 12 shillings; and for the nail the compensation shall be 2 shillings.

59. If the ring finger (gold-finger) be struck off, for that (to þam) 17 shillings must *be paid* in compensation; and for the nail, 4 shillings compensation.

60. If the little finger is struck off, for that he must *pay* 9 shillings compensation, and one shilling for the nail if that is struck off.

61. If someone is wounded in the belly (hrif), let *the aggressor pay* 30 shillings in compensation; if the wound goes through *the body* (he þurh-wund bið), *let him pay* 20 shillings for each opening (muðe).

62. If someone's thigh or hip (þeoh) is perforated (þyrel), let *the aggressor* pay him 30 shillings in compensation. If it be disabled (forad), the compensation (bot) will also be 30 shillings.

63. If the leg be pierced (þyrel) below the knee, in that case 12 shillings must *be paid* in compensation. If he is disabled (forad) below the knee, let *the aggressor* give him 30 shillings in compensation.

64. If the great toe is struck off, let *the aggressor* give him 20 shillings in compensation.

    If it is the second toe, let *the aggressor* give him 15 shillings compensation.

    If the middle toe is struck off, then 9 shillings must *be paid* in compensation.

    If it is the fourth toe, then 6 shillings must *be paid* in compensation.

    If the little toe is struck off, let *the aggressor* give him 5 shillings.

65. If someone is so severely wounded in the testicles (herðan) that he cannot bear children, let *the aggressor* compensate him with 80 shillings.

66. If a man's arm complete with the hand is cut off below the elbow, let *the aggressor* compensate him with 80 shillings.

    For every wound before the hair-*line* and below the sleeve and below the knee, let the compensation be twice the value (twy sceatte mare).

67. If the loins (lenden-bræde) are permanently damaged (forslegen), then 60 shillings must *be paid* in compensation; if they are stabbed (on bestungen), let *the aggressor* give 15 shillings as compensation; if they are pierced right through (þurh-þyrel), then in that case must 30 shillings *be paid* in compensation.

68. If someone is wounded (wund) in the shoulder, let *the aggressor* pay compensation (gebete) of 80 shillings – if the man *i.e. the victim* be alive.[97]

69. If someone maim (forslea) another's hand outwardly (utan), let him give 20 shillings as compensation, providing (gif) it can be treated effectively (mon gelacnian mæge). If half the hand be lost (onweg flioge), then 40 shillings must *be paid* in compensation.

70. If someone break (forslea) another's rib without breaking his skin (binnan gehalre hyde), let *the aggressor* give 10 shillings in compensation; if the skin is broken (tobrocen) and the bone be extruded (man ban of-ado). let him give 15 shillings in compensation.

71. If someone cut away (of-aslea) another man's eye or hand or foot, there applies (gæð) a similar compensation in all cases: 6 pennies and six shillings and 60 shillings and the third part of a penny.

72. If someone's leg be cut off (ofaslagen) at the knee, then 80 shillings must *be paid* in compensation.

---

[97] This final qualifier raises the perhaps obvious point, that if someone dies from a wound (but over what period?), then the lesser penalty yields to the full wergeld.

73. If someone break (forslea) another man's shoulder, let *the aggressor* give him 20 shillings in compensation.

74. If someone hack (in-beslea) into it *i.e. the shoulder*, and makes the bone extrude (mon ban of-ado), let *the aggressor* give him 15 shillings in compensation.

75. If someone sever (forslea) the tendon of the foot (greatan sinwe), *and* if it can be treated (mon gelacnian mæge) so that will be sound (hal) again, let *the aggressor* pay 12 shillings in compensation. *But* if the man is lame (healt) on account of the wound and he cannot be cured, let *the aggressor* pay 30 shillings in compensation.

76. If the lesser tendon (smalan sinwe)[98] be severed (mon forslea), let *the aggressor* pay 6 shillings in compensation.

77. If someone sever (forslea) the muscles (geweald) up by the neck, and damage (forwundie) them so severely that he *i.e. the victim* has no control (geweald) over them, and however lives on thus maimed (swa gescended), let *the aggressor* give him 100 shillings in compensation, unless the Witan appoint (gereccan) him a juster (ryhtre) and greater (mare) *sum*.

---

[98] Perhaps also in the foot, but not certainly so.

EDMUND

[Despite a reversal at the start of his reign, Edmund, king 939–946, continued the military and political achievements of his predecessors, Alfred, Edward and Athelstan (his older brother), and arguably in his reign the influence of Wessex, as the leader of the confederation we call England, reached its highest point.

The law-code translated here is a Latin one, though only because the Old English original is no longer extant, for the phrasing is taken to show that a vernacular text once lay behind the Latin.[1] It shows a political will and audacity in keeping with the military supremacy of Wessex, and though the most of its provisions refer to theft, it contains some wide-ranging powers that might be used in almost any context, including the right to exact support for the centralised justice system, which seems a change from the previous assumption of the free-man as the standard of regulation and thus in some sense the focus of the law.

Most obvious is the opening provision for a national oath of allegiance, a forerunner to the more elegant coronation oath of Edgar,[2] that bound monarch to people in a joint loyalty. Here the action is one-way, and the citizen is to be committed without reservation to a personification of power and law in the figure of the king, whose role is now amplified in an enlarged kingdom. Law-breaking becomes altogether an offence against the Crown, rather than against the person, and the subsequent provisions deal with one after another loop-hole by which evasion of penalty had been sought.]

This is the decree (institutio) which King Edmund and his bishops and his councillors (sapientibus) established at Colyton (apud Culintonam)

---

[1] See for example Robertson's notes, pp.298–9, and refs. to Liebermann there. The Latin is Post-Conquest for example using Norman-Latin like 'barganniet'.

[2] Coronation oaths were also in use in Germany in the 10th century; see Kern p.76.

regarding *the king's* peace (de pace) and the swearing of an oath *of allegiance.*

1. Firstly, that everyone should swear, in the name of God (Domini), to whom this sacred thing (sanctum)[3] is holy, loyalty (fidalitatem) to King Edmund, in the way it is proper for a man to be faithful to his lord, without any dispute (controversia) or deceit (seductione) in public or private, but cherishing (amando) what he will cherish, and rejecting (nolendo) what he will reject; and from the day (a die – emendation to text) on which this oath is given, let no one conceal *a breach*[4] of it in a brother or a neighbour (proximo) any more than in a stranger (extraneo).

2. Further it is his will that where a thief (fur) is certainly revealed, nobles (twelfhindi) and commoners (twihindi) shall join in capturing him, alive or dead, whichever they can; and let him that declares a feud (infaidiabit) against anyone who took part in that search be deemed an enemy of the king and of all his friends;[5] and let him that refuses *to join such a venture* or fails (nolit) to help, pay 120 shillings to the king and 30 shillings to the Hundred – or deny that he knew *what was happening* by an equivalent oath.

3. And it is my will that no one receive another *into his service* before there is a settlement (quietus) regarding anyone who might seek justice (rectum) from him *i.e. the new-comer*; and he that protects and supports (manutenebit et firmavit) anyone who commits an offence (ad dampnum), shall be responsible for his custody and for producing him to pay compensation (ad emendandum), or shall himself be liable to pay what the other should have paid.[6]

4. And it is pronounced with regard to slaves (de servis) that if a group of them commit theft, the leader (senior) of them shall be

---

[3] Presumably an altar.

[4] What is not to be concealed is not explicit in the Latin; it might be non-swearing of the oath that is meant, for example.

[5] The idea seems to be, that anyone who tries to avenge someone killed 'during arrest' should be outlawed.

[6] It is not entirely clear here whether any secular lord is made liable for the acts of a retainer, or only if he has taken on a man of bad character or supported him in wrong-doing. cf. chapter 7, below, which is more explicit.

captured and executed (occidatur[7]) or hanged, and each of the others shall be flogged three times and scalped (extoppentur[8]) and the little finger shall be cut off as a *permanent* sign.

5. And no one shall make a deal (barganniet) for or take in cattle of unknown origin (ignotum pecus) unless he has the witness of a shire reeve (summi praepositi) or a priest or a *royal* steward (hordarii) or a port-reeve.[9]

6. And it is pronounced concerning the tracking and searching for stolen cattle that investigation shall be made in the locality (ad villam) and there shall be no obstacle or any hindrance to the pursuit or search. And if the trail[10] does not lead out of that region (de terra), let search be made wherever suspicion or doubt exists *within the locality.* And if anyone there is accused, let him clear himself in an appropriate manner, and let the *evidence of the trail* stand for the prosecution (pro superjuramento); and anyone who thwarts (prohibebit) a search of this kind shall pay the value *of the animals to the owner* and 120 shillings to the king; and anyone who abstains or refuses help or is unwilling to see justice done shall pay 120 shillings to the king.

7. And every master (homo) shall act as surety (credibiles faciat) for his men and for everyone who is under his protection (in pace) or on his land (terra). And all those of ill-repute or charged with a number of offences shall be required to find a pledge (sub plegio redigantur).[11] And the reeve (praepositus) or thane (tainus) or nobleman (comes) or commoner (villanus) who is unwilling to do so or fails to do so shall pay *a fine of* 120 shillings and incur the penalties stated above.[12]

---

7 The Latin word may have implications of death by sword stroke.

8 Baxter's *Medieval Latin Word-List* gives also 'to shave' as a meaning of this verb, but that hardly seems to fit the seriousness of the rest the punishment; for other references to scalping see Robertson p.299.

9 i.e. so that the cattle can be located if any claim later arise.

10 A rare example of the role of physical evidence in solving crime.

11 I take this to mean, that a sort of financial guarantee has to be actually posted in such a case.

12 But not in the surviving version of the text.

ÆTHELRED

[To conclude, I cite the fragment 10 Ethelred, datable to 1009–16, a period of almost unrelieved Viking pressure on England, when it became essential to maintain the institutions of government and national unity (not always compatible: the St Brice's Day massacre of 1002 shows Ethelred using royal power to create divisive anti-Danish feeling; while the prosecution of Wulfnoth in 1009 led to the defection of much of Ethelred's fleet).

The Old English text has many word-pairs, often alliterating, which are taken to indicate the authorship of Wulfstan, Archbishop of York, who endeavoured not only to bring (moral) order to the laws of Ethelred but similarly to those of Cnut in the following period. His abstract and emphatic style may have gone some way to reassuring the thinkers of his time, but the complex and discouraging political and military conditions of the time could not be easily legislated away.

It must remain uncertain whether this is a fragment of a full law-code, a partial text of some reaffirmation (with minor additions or alterations, or special application) of the Enham code, or some draft for royal consideration that evidences Wulfstan's industry rather than settled law. In any case, it is the theoretical emphasis of the text that is notable, as though Law has become a moral force, which could be used to spread ideas and influence attitudes. Practical, detailed provisions may have followed on, but pride of place is given to refined analysis which echoes but also transcends the emphasis Alfred placed on Christianity as the unifying bond of the nation and its law.]

There is one eternal God, the ruler and maker of all creation (ealra gesceafta); and in honour of his name I, King Ethelred, have been considering first how I could continue best to promote Christianity and just secular authority (rihtne cynedom), and how I could most usefully define my own role (me sylfum gerædan[1]) in

---

[1] Robertson translates: "could determine with the greatest profit to myself".

religious and secular matters (for Gode and for worolde) and most
justly legislate (rihtlicast lagian) for all my subjects (leodscype) such
measures (þa þing) as *it is* necessary (to þearfe) we must observe.

1. It has come to my mind repeatedly that holy canons (lara) and wise
secular laws (worold-laga) promote Christianity (cristendom) and
strengthen (micliað) royal authority (cynedom), benefit the people
(folce) and lead to distinction (weorðscypes wealdað[2]), unite and
conciliate and settle divisions and improve the whole morality
(þeawas) of the nation (þeode).

2. Now it is my will eagerly to explore (spyrian) how we may best
maintain canons and laws and entirely remove all injustice
(unlaga).

3. And this is the law-code (gerædnes) that it is our will be observed,
in accordance with what we firmly decreed (fæste gecwædon) at
Enham.[3]

4. That is, firstly, that we all keenly turn from sin and eagerly make
amends (betan) for our misdeeds, and always love and worship the
one God and keenly uphold Christianity and entirely renounce all
pagan customs (hæðendom).

5. And the decree (gerædnes) of the Witan is that we should uphold
just laws and keenly suppress all injustice (unlaga), and that we
allow everyone access to the law (rihtes wyrðe); and that we
properly maintain peace (frið) and concord (freondscype) in
religious and secular matters....

---

[2] A rhetorical phrase, perhaps equivalent to 'bring success'.
[3] i.e. 5 Ethelred.

READING GUIDE

ATTENBOROUGH, F. L. *The Laws of the Earliest English Kings* (Cambridge 1922).
Text and translation.

BYRNE, Francis J. *Irish Kings and High Kings* (London 1973).
Some notes on Irish Laws, pp.31–38.

COLLINS, Roger 'Theodebert I, Rex Magnus Francorum'
pp.7–33 in *Ideal and Reality in Frankish and Anglo-Saxon Society: Studies presented to J M Wallace-Hadrill* ed. Patrick Wormald (Oxford, 1983).
Relates sixth century law-codes in Britain and Europe to Church influence, aiming to reform secular power in line with late Roman models.

CROOK, J. A. *Law and Life of Rome* (London, 1967).
General account from Institutes of Gaius (2nd century AD) to Justinian.

DAMMERY, Richard J. E. The Law-Code of King Alfred the Great. PhD, Cambridge, 1990 (2 vols.).
Vol.1, introduction, considers probability that rubrics (list of headings) are not original to the law-code, and therefore connection of Alfred's laws with those of Ine may not have been intended by Alfred himself. Vol.2 is a collated text, based on CCCC173.

DAVIS, H. W. C. "The Anglo-Saxon Laws" *EHR* 28 (!913) 417–430.
A consideration of Liebermann's career and edition of the Laws.

DREW, Katherine F. (trans.) *The Burgundian Code* (Philadelphia, 1972).
Introduction and Text.

DREW, Katherine F. Law and Society in Early Medieval Europe (London, 1988).
Especially item 'Barbarian Kings as Lawgivers and Judges', which surveys early post-Roman Latin law-codes.

DUMVILLE, David N. 'On the Dating of Early Breton Law-codes'
Item XI in *Britons and Anglo-Saxons in the Early Middle Ages*
(Aldershot, 1993, originally published separately 1984).
In Breton secular Laws ('Excerpta de Libris Romanorum et
Francorum') are conventionally dated to mid sixth century, but might
be safer assigned to eighth century.

ECKHARDT, Karl A. Leges Anglo-Saxonum 601–925 (Göttingen,
1958).
Texts of laws and translation into German, with parallel Latin
(Quadripartitum) text – cf. Schmidt, 1858. Glossary, but no real
notes.

GOEBEL, Julius Jr. *Felony and Misdemeanor: A study in the history
of criminal law* (1937, reissued Pennsylvania 1976).
General survey of theory and practice of law on the continent from
Merovingian to feudal times, with some reference to England (esp.
ch.6).

HUGHES, Kathleen *Early Christian Ireland: Introduction to the
sources* (London, 1972).
Especially chapter 2, on the secular laws, which were in force
seventh to eighth century, though written down later. "They are in no
sense the king's law, but statements of customary practice" (p.43);
"There was no royal laws or administration... there was no central
government for day-to-day affairs" (p.53).

KENNEDY, A. G. 'Cnut's Law Code of 1018' *Anglo-Saxon England*
11 (1983) 57–81.
Introduction, text and translation of a version of VI Æthelred
compiled by Wulfstan and studied especially by Whitelock.

KERN, F. (trans. S. B. Chrimes) *Kingship and Law in the Middle Ages*
(Oxford, 1939).
Originally published in German in 1914; a wide survey of the
development of European kingship; plus a briefer, more abstract
essay on Law.

KEYNES, Simon and LAPIDGE, Michael (trans.) *Alfred the Great*
(Middlesex, 1983).
Collection of source texts in translation, including some of Alfred's
Laws (pp.163–170), and Fulco's Letter (pp.182–186)

KIRBY, D. P. *The Making of Early England* (London, 1967).
Includes useful introduction to kinship and law, pp.140–150.

KIRBY, D. P. *The Earliest English Kings* (London, 1991).
References to each of the early law-codes; queries Bede's
information (*HE* II,5) that Ethelberht ruled 56 years.

LIEBERMANN, F. *Die Gesetze der Angelsachsen* (3 vols., Halle
1903–1916).
Vol.1 (1903) gives text and (German) translation; vol.2 (1906) is a
glossary; vol.3 (1916) is notes.

LIEBERMANN, F. 'Notes on the Textus Roffensis' *Archaeologia
Cantiana* 23 (1898) 101–112.
Concludes Textus Roffensis not a compilation of the 12th century,
but a copy of a collection of laws of ca.1000 AD, perhaps from
Canterbury, which would already have contained the Kentish Laws.

LOYN, Bruce *A Constitutional and Legal History of Medieval England*
(NY, 1960).
Wide coverage of information; though from a conventionally
authoritarian viewpoint.

LOYN, Henry *Society and Peoples: Studies in the History of England
and Wales, ca.600–1200* (London, 1992).
A collection of essays covering especially customary law, kin and
local institutions.

MAITLAND, F. W. 'History of English Law' – item 5 in *Selected
Historical Essays of F. W. Maitland* (Cambridge, 1957).
Suggests Ethelberht's Laws may have been inspired by Justinian's
legislation ca.600; Alfred's and later laws may owe something to
Frankish Capitularies; but in general no influence from Roman Law.

MUIRHEAD, Professor and **GOUDY, Henry** 'Roman Law' – entry in
Encyclopaedia Britannica, 11th edn., 1910–11.

Extensive discussion of concept and practice of Roman Law, down
to Justinian. Distinguishes two strands in early Roman Law – *fas*,
"the will of the gods, the laws given by heaven for men on earth" –
and *jus*, human law, either customary or statute (*lex*). While early
Roman law included approval by plebiscite or legislation by the
comitia (general electoral assembly), after Diocletian's time, even

the involvement of the Senate was dispensed with, and the promulgation of law was exclusively in the hands of the emperors.

NELSON, Janet 'Legislation and Consensus in the Reign of Charles the Bald' pp.202–227 in *Ideal and Reality in Frankish and Anglo-Saxon Society: Studies presented to J M Wallace-Hadrill* ed. Patrick Wormald (Oxford, 1983).
Notes the importance of churchmen as drafters of laws in the case of the mid 9th century Capitularies of Charles the Bald.

RICHARDS, Mary P. 'The Manuscript Contexts of the Old English Laws: Tradition and innovation' pp.171–192 in *Studies in Earlier Old English Prose* ed. Paul E. Szarmach (Albany, N.Y., 1986). Useful survey of the six principle MSS, emphasising that the preferred written order was from current to past, and that earlier codes were used to supplement more recent law-codes in practice.

RICHARDS, Mary P. 'Elements of a written standard in the Old English Laws' pp.1–22 in *Standardising English* (J. H. Fisher festschrift) ed. J. B. Trahern Jr., (Tennessee Studies in Literature no.31, Knoxille, 1989).

ROBERTSON, A. J. (ed./trans.) *The Laws of the Kings of England from Edmund to Henry I* (Cambridge 1925) [IHR].
Companion volume to Attenborough's.

SCHMIDT, Reinhold *Die Gesetze der Angelsachsen.* Leipzig, 1858.
Old English texts, plus German translation and Latin Quadripartitus, up to Henry I.

SISAM, Kenneth *Studies in the History of Old English Literature* (Oxford, 1953).
Contains two items of interest: 'The Authenticity of Certain texts in Lambard's *Archaionomia*' and a note on 'The Relationship of Ethelred's Codes V and VI', suggesting that 6 Ethelred is a version "for parish priests in the province of York."

SIMPSON, A. W. B. *The Laws of Ethelbert* pp.3–17 in *On the Laws and Customs of England: Essays in honor of Samuel E. Thorne* ed. M. S. Arnold et al. (North Carolina, 1981).
Includes analysis of the structure of the law-code.

THORPE, Benjamin (ed./trans.) *Ancient Laws and Institutes of England* (2 vols., London 1840).
Text and translation. Vol.1 covers the secular laws, vol.2 ecclesiastical laws plus Quadripartitus (Latin version) and glossary.

WALLACE-HADRILL, J. M. *Early Germanic Kingship in England and on the Continent* (Oxford, 1971).
Statement of the development of kingship and the concepts behind it.

WHITELOCK, Dorothy 'Wulfstan and the so-called Laws of Edward *and* Guthrum' *English Historical Review* 56 (1941) 1–21.
Analyses this set of ecclesiastical legislation and attributes it to Wulfstan.

WHITELOCK, Dorothy 'Wulfstan and the Laws of Cnut' *English Historical Review* 63 (1948) 433–452.
Considers an abstract of Ethelred's Laws which are shown to be preparatory work for Cnut's law-code, and attributable to Wulfstan ca.1018.

WHITELOCK, Dorothy 'The Law', chapter 7 in her book *The Beginnings of. English Society* (Middlesex, 1952).
Careful wide-ranging account.

WHITELOCK, Dorothy 'Wulfstan's Authorship of Cnut's Laws' *English Historical Review* 70 (1955) 72–85.
Further analyses the transitional text she wrote about in 1948 as "a set of extracts from VI Ethelred, to which some material from other sources has been appended" (p.73), and confirms it as evidence that Wulfstan composed Cnut's Laws. 6 Ethelred is confirmed as a Danelaw version itself compiled by Wulfstan from 5 Ethelred.

WHITELOCK, Dorothy (ed.) *English Historical Documents I. ca.500–1042* (London, 1955).
Large collection of source material in translation including selected law-codes e.g. Ethelbert, Wihtred, Ine, Alfred etc., up to Cnut.

WITNEY, K. P. *The Kingdom of Kent* (London, 1982).
Detailed study including analysis of Kentish Laws.

WORMALD, Patrick "Æthelred the Lawmaker" pp.47–80 in *Ethelred the Unready: Papers from the Millenary Conference* ed. David Hill (British Archaeological Reports, British Series, no. 59, 1978).

General account, which emphasises the oral nature of law as against the written versions.

WORMALD, Patrick '*Lex Scripta* and *Verbum Regis*: Legislation and Germanic kingship, from Euric to Cnut' pp.105–138 in *Early Medieval Kingship*, ed. P. H. Sawyer and I. N. Wood (Leeds, 1977) Emphasising royal and abstract nature of Laws.

YORKE, Barbara *Kings and Kingdoms of Early Anglo-Saxon England* (London, 1990).
Includes notes on Ethelberht's and Ine's law-codes.

Some of our other titles

An Introduction to the Old English Language and its Literature
Stephen Pollington

The purpose of this general introduction to Old English is not to deal with the teaching of Old English but to dispel some misconceptions about the language and to give an outline of its structure and its literature. Some basic knowledge about the origins of the English language and its early literature is essential to an understanding of the early period of English history and the present form of the language. This revised and expanded edition provides a useful guide for those contemplating embarking on a linguistic journey.

£4.95   A5   ISBN 1-898281-06-8   64 pages

First Steps in Old English
An easy to follow language course for the beginner
Stephen Pollington

A complete, well presented and easy to use Old English language course that contains all the exercises and texts needed to learn Old English. This course has been designed to be of help to a wide range of students, from those who are teaching themselves at home, to undergraduates who are learning Old English as part of their English degree course. The author is aware that some individuals have little aptitude for learning languages and that many have difficulty with grammar. To help overcome these problems he has adopted a step-by-step approach that enables students of differing abilities to advance at their own pace. The course includes many exercises designed to aid the learning process. A correspondence course is also available.

£16.95   ISBN 1-898281-19-X   9½" x 6¾"/245 x 170mm   224 pages

Ærgeweorc: Old English Verse and Prose read by Stephen Pollington

This audiotape cassette can be used in conjunction with *First Steps in Old English* or just listened to for the sheer pleasure of hearing Old English spoken well.
Tracks: 1. Deor. 2. Beowulf – The Funeral of Scyld Scefing. 3. Engla Tocyme (The Arrival of the English). 4. Ines Domas. Two Extracts from the Laws of King Ine. 5. Deniga Hergung (The Danes' Harrying) Anglo-Saxon Chronicle Entry AD997. 6. Durham 7. The Ordeal (Be ðon ðe ordales weddigaþ) 8. Wið Dweorh (Against a Dwarf) 9. Wið Wennum (Against Wens) 10. Wið Wæterælfadle (Against Waterelf Sickness) 11. The Nine Herbs Charm 12. Læcedomas (Leechdoms) 13. Beowulf's Greeting 14. The Battle of Brunanburh 15. Blacmon – by Adrian Pilgrim.

£7.50   ISBN 1-898281-20-3   C40 audiotape   Old English transcript supplied with tape.

Wordcraft: Concise English/Old English Dictionary and Thesaurus
Stephen Pollington

Wordcraft provides Old English equivalents to the commoner modern words in both dictionary and thesaurus formats. Previously the lack of an accessible guide to vocabulary deterred many would-be students of Old English. *Wordcraft* combines the core of indispensable words relating to everyday life with a selection of terms connected with society, culture, technology, religion, perception, emotion and expression to encompass all aspects of Anglo-Saxon experience. The Thesaurus presents vocabulary relevant to a wide range of individual topics in alphabetical lists, thus making it easily accessible to those with specific areas of interest. Each thematic listing is encoded for cross-reference from the Dictionary. The two sections will be of invaluable assistance to students of the language, as well as those with either a general or a specific interest in the Anglo-Saxon period.

£9.95   ISBN 1-898281-02-5   A5   256 pages

Leechcraft: Early English Charms, Plantlore and Healing
Stephen Pollington

An unequalled examination of every aspect of early English healing, including the use of plants, amulets, charms, and prayer. Other topics covered include Anglo-Saxon witchcraft; tree-lore; gods, elves and dwarves.

The author has brought together a wide range of evidence for the English healing tradition, and presented it in a clear and readable manner. The extensive 2,000-entry index makes it possible for the reader to quickly find specific information.

The three key Old English texts are reproduced in full, accompanied by new translations. *Bald's Third Leechbook*; *Lacnunga*; *Old English Herbarium*.

£35 ISBN 1–898281–23–8 10" x 6¾" (254 x 170mm) hard bk 28 illustrations 544 pages

A Guide to Late Anglo-Saxon England: From Alfred to Eadgar II 871–1074
Donald Henson

This guide has been prepared with the aim of providing the general readers with both an overview of the period and a wealth of background information. Facts and figures are presented in a way that makes this a useful reference handbook.

Contents include: The Origins of England; Physical Geography; Human Geography; English Society; Government and Politics; The Church; Language and Literature; Personal Names; Effects of the Norman Conquest. All of the kings from Alfred to Eadgar II are dealt with separately and there is a chronicle of events for each of their reigns. There are also maps, family trees and extensive appendices.

£9.95 ISBN 1–898281–21–1 9½" x 6¾"/245 x 170mm, 6 maps & 3 family trees 208 pages

The English Elite in 1066 - Gone but not forgotten
Donald Henson

The people listed in this book formed the topmost section of the ruling elite in 1066. It includes all those who held office between the death of Eadward III (January 1066) and the abdication of Eadgar II (December 1066). There are 455 individuals in the main entries and these have been divided according to their office or position.

The following information is listed where available:
- What is known of their life;
- Their landed wealth;
- The early sources in which information about the individual can be found
- Modern references that give details about his or her life.

In addition to the biographical details, there is a wealth of background information about English society and government. A series of appendices provide detailed information about particular topics or groups of people.

£16.95 ISBN 1–898281–26–2 250 x 175mm / 10 x 7 inches 272 pages

Looking for the Lost Gods of England
Kathleen Herbert

Kathleen Herbert sifts through the royal genealogies, charms, verse and other sources to find clues to the names and attributes of the Gods and Goddesses of the early English. The earliest account of English heathen practices reveals that they worshipped the Earth Mother and called her Nerthus. The tales, beliefs and traditions of that time are still with us and able to stir our minds and imaginations.

£4.95   ISBN 1–898281–04–1   A5   64 pages

A Handbook of Anglo-Saxon Food: Processing and Consumption
Ann Hagen

For the first time information from various sources has been brought together in order to build up a picture of how food was grown, conserved, prepared and eaten during the period from the beginning of the 5th century to the 11th century. No specialist knowledge of the Anglo-Saxon period or language is needed, and many people will find it fascinating for the views it gives of an important aspect of Anglo-Saxon life and culture. In addition to Anglo-Saxon England the Celtic west of Britain is also covered. Subject headings include: drying, milling and bread making; dairying; butchery; preservation and storage; methods of cooking; meals and mealtimes; fasting; feasting; food shortages and deficiency diseases.

£9.95   ISBN 0–9516209–8–3   A5   192 pages

A Second Handbook of Anglo-Saxon Food & Drink
Production & Distribution
Ann Hagen

This second handbook complements the first and brings together a vast amount of information. Subject headings include: cereal crops; vegetables, herbs and fungi; fruit and nuts; cattle; sheep; goats; pigs; poultry and eggs; wild animals and birds; honey; fish and molluscs; imported food; tabooed food; provision of a water supply; fermented drinks; hospitality and charity. 27-page index.

Food production for home consumption was the basis of economic activity throughout the Anglo-Saxon period and ensuring access to an adequate food supply was a constant preoccupation. Used as payment and a medium of trade, food was the basis of the Anglo-Saxons' system of finance and administration.

£14.95   ISBN 1–898281–12–2   A5   432 pages

Anglo-Saxon Riddles
Translated by John Porter

This is a book full of ingenious characters who speak their names in riddles. Here you will meet a one-eyed garlic seller, a bookworm, an iceberg, an oyster, the sun and moon and a host of others from the everyday life and imagination of the Anglo-Saxons.

John Porter's sparkling translations retain all the vigour and subtly of the original Old English poems, transporting us back over a thousand years to the roots of our language and literature.

Contains all 95 riddles of the Exeter Book in Old English with Modern English translations.

£4.95   ISBN 1–898281–32–7   A5   112 pages

Rudiments of Runelore

Stephen Pollington

The purpose of this book is to provide both a comprehensive introduction for those coming to the subject for the first time, and a handy and inexpensive reference work for those with some knowledge of the subject. The *Abecedarium Nordmannicum* and the English, Norwegian and Icelandic rune poems are included as are two rune riddles, extracts from the Cynewulf poems and new work on the three Brandon runic inscriptions and the Norfolk 'Tiw' runes.

Headings include: The Origin of the Runes; Runes among the Germans; The Germanic Rune Row and the Common Germanic Language; The English Runic Tradition; The Scandinavian Runic Tradition; Runes and Pseudo-runes; The Use of Runes; Bind Runes and Runic Cryptography.

£4.95   ISBN 1–898281–16–5   A5   Illustrations   96 pages

Rune Cards

Brian Partridge & Tony Linsell

> "This boxed set of 30 cards contains some of the most beautiful and descriptive black and white line drawings that I have ever seen on this subject."
>
> *Pagan News*

30 pen and ink drawings by Brian Partridge
80 page booklet by Tony Linsell gives information about the origin of runes, their meaning, and how to read them.

£9.95   ISBN 1-898281-34-3   30 cards & 80 page booklet - boxed

English Sea Power 871-1100AD

John Pullen-Appleby

This work examines the largely untold story of English sea power prior to the Norman Conquest. The author illuminates the much-neglected period 871 to 1100, an age when English rulers deployed naval resources, first against Norse Invaders, and later as an instrument of state in relations with neighbouring countries.

The author has gathered together information about the crewing, appearance and use of fighting ships during the period.

£14.95   ISBN 1-898281-31-9   9 ¾ x 6 ¾ inches   248 x 170mm   128 pages

Ordering   Please check latest prices before ordering.

Payment may be made by Visa, or Mastercard. Telephone orders accepted.

Payment may also be made by a cheque drawn on a UK bank in sterling.

If you are paying by cheque please make it payable to Anglo-Saxon Books and enclose it with your order. When ordering by post please write clearly.

UK deliveries add 10% up to a maximum of £2· 50

Europe – including **Republic of Ireland** - add 10% plus £1 – all orders sent airmail

North America add 10% surface delivery, 30% airmail

Elsewhere add 10% surface delivery, 40% airmail

Overseas surface delivery 5–8 weeks; airmail 5–10 days

For details of other titles and our North American distributor see our website or contact us at:

Anglo-Saxon Books

Frithgarth, Thetford Forest Park, Hockwold-cum-Wilton, Norfolk IP26 4NQ
web site: www.asbooks.co.uk   e-mail: enq@asbooks.co.uk
Tel: 01842 828430   Fax: 01842 828332

Organisations

Þa Engliscan Gesiðas

Þa Engliscan Gesiðas (The English Companions) is a historical and cultural society exclusively devoted to Anglo-Saxon history. Its aims are to bridge the gap between scholars and non-experts, and to bring together all those with an interest in the Anglo-Saxon period, its language, culture and traditions, so as to promote a wider interest in, and knowledge of all things Anglo-Saxon. The Fellowship publishes a journal, *Wiðowinde,* which helps members to keep in touch with current thinking on topics from art and archaeology to heathenism and Early English Christianity. The Fellowship enables like-minded people to keep in contact by publicising conferences, courses and meetings that might be of interest to its members.

For further details see www.kami.demon.co.uk/gesithas/ or write to: The Membership Secretary, Þa Engliscan Gesiðas, BM Box 4336, London, WC1N 3XX England.

Regia Anglorum

Regia Anglorum was founded to accurately re-create the life of the British people as it was around the time of the Norman Conquest. Our work has a strong educational slant. We consider authenticity to be of prime importance and prefer, where possible, to work from archaeological materials. Approximately twenty-five per cent of our members, of over 500 people, are archaeologists or historians.

The Society has a large working Living History Exhibit, teaching and exhibiting more than twenty crafts in an authentic environment. We own a forty-foot wooden ship replica of a type that would have been a common sight in Northern European waters around the turn of the first millennium AD. Battle re-enactment is another aspect of our activities, often involving 200 or more warriors.

For further information see www.regia.org or contact: K. J. Siddorn, 9 Durleigh Close, Headley Park, Bristol BS13 7NQ, England, e-mail: kim_siddorn@compuserve.com

The Sutton Hoo Society

Our aims and objectives focus on promoting research and education relating to the Anglo Saxon Royal cemetery at Sutton Hoo, Suffolk in the UK. The Society publishes a newsletter SAXON twice a year, which keeps members up to date with society activities, carries resumes of lectures and visits, and reports progress on research and publication associated with the site. If you would like to join the Society please write to:

Membership Secretary, Sutton Hoo Society,
258 The Pastures, High Wycombe, Buckinghamshire HP13 5RS England
website: www.suttonhoo.org

Wuffing Education

Wuffing Education provides those interested in the history, archaeology, literature and culture of the Anglo-Saxons with the chance to meet experts and fellow enthusiasts for a whole day of in-depth seminars and discussions. Day Schools take place at the historic Tranmer House overlooking the burial mounds of Sutton Hoo in Suffolk.

For details of programme of events contact:-
Wuffing Education, 4 Hilly Fields, Woodbridge, Suffolk IP12 4DX
email education@wuffings.co.uk   website www.wuffings.co.uk
Tel. 01394 383908 or 01728 688749

Places to visit

Bede's World at Jarrow

Bede's world tells the remarkable story of the life and times of the Venerable Bede, 673–735 AD. Visitors can explore the origins of early medieval Northumbria and Bede's life and achievements through his own writings and the excavations of the monasteries at Jarrow and other sites.

Location – 10 miles from Newcastle upon Tyne, off the A19 near the southern entrance to the River Tyne tunnel. Bus services 526 & 527

Bede's World, Church Bank, Jarrow, Tyne and Wear, NE32 3DY
Tel. 0191 489 2106; Fax: 0191 428 2361; website: www.bedesworld.co.uk

Sutton Hoo near Woodbridge, Suffolk

Sutton Hoo is a group of low burial mounds overlooking the River Deben in south-east Suffolk. Excavations in 1939 brought to light the richest burial ever discovered in Britain – an Anglo-Saxon ship containing a magnificent treasure which has become one of the principal attractions of the British Museum. The mound from which the treasure was dug is thought to be the grave of Rædwald, an early English king who died in 624/5 AD.

This National Trust site has an excellent visitor centre, which includes a reconstruction of the burial chamber and its grave goods. Some original objects as well as replicas of the treasure are on display.

2 miles east of Woodbridge on B1083   Tel. 01394 389700

West Stow Anglo-Saxon Village

An early Anglo-Saxon Settlement reconstructed on the site where it was excavated consisting of timber and thatch hall, houses and workshop. There is also a museum containing objects found during the excavation of the site. Open all year 10am–4.15pm (except Yuletide). Special provision for school parties. A teachers' resource pack is available. Costumed events are held on some weekends, especially Easter Sunday and August Bank Holiday Monday. Craft courses are organised.

For further details see www.stedmunds.co.uk/west_stow.html or contact:
The Visitor Centre, West Stow Country Park, Icklingham Road, West Stow,
Bury St Edmunds, Suffolk IP28 6HG   Tel. 01284 728718